CULTURE SMART!

FINLAND

THE ESSENTIAL GUIDE TO
CUSTOMS & CULTURE

TERTTU LENEY AND ELENA BARRETT

KUPERARD

"The real voyage of discovery consists not in seeking new landscapes, but in having new eyes."

Adapted from Marcel Proust, *Remembrance of Things Past.*

ISBN 978 1 78702 908 8

British Library Cataloguing in Publication Data
A CIP catalogue entry for this book is available
from the British Library

First published in Great Britain
by Kuperard, an imprint of Bravo Ltd
59 Hutton Grove, London N12 8DS
Tel: +44 (0) 20 8446 2440
www.culturesmart.co.uk
Inquiries: publicity@kuperard.co.uk

Design Bobby Birchall
Printed in Turkey

ABOUT THE AUTHOR

TERTTU LENEY was a Finnish teacher, trainer, broadcaster, and writer, who worked for the Foreign Office in London as a professional development coordinator preparing British diplomats and businessmen for overseas postings. A graduate in Russian and Swedish language and literature from the School of Slavonic and East European Studies, University of London, she went on to complete a postgraduate diploma in language training at the University of Westminster and write several publications, including *Teach Yourself Finnish*, *Finn Talk 1*, and *Finn Talk 2*.

ELENA BARRETT is a teacher, writer, applied linguist, and long-time resident of Finland. Originally from Connecticut, USA, she has taught English to Finnish adults and upper-secondary students. She is presently finishing her studies and researching language use in legal contexts at the University of Jyväskylä, Finland. She has also maintained a blog about her life as an immigrant in Finland called *Already There*.

CONTENTS

MAP OF FINLAND

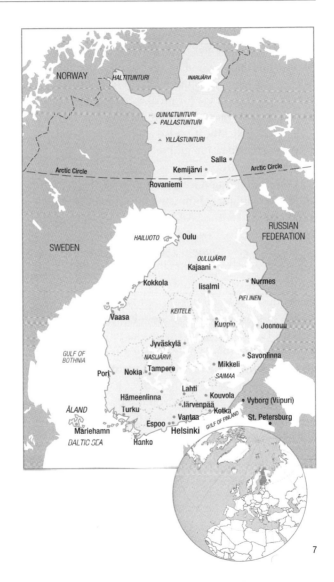

Finland is something like a Nordic paradise; it is the land of white summer nights, of white Christmases and Santa Claus, and of a thousand pristine lakes. It contains kilometers upon kilometers of forest, where one can forage for mushrooms and berries, or simply bask in the scent of pine under the towering trees. Paradoxically, it is also a land of modernity and innovation, education and technology, and increasing cultural diversity.

Finns have fought long and hard for the right to their own, uniquely Finnish cultural identity. As politician and author Adolf Ivar Arwidsson famously said, "*Ruotsalaisia emme enää ole, venäläisiksi emme tahdo tulla, olkaamme siis suomalaisia,*" or, "We are no longer Swedes, we do not wish to become Russians, so let us be Finns." This quote sums up neatly the desire for Finnishness, and the desire to carve out a space in which Finns are free to be, well, Finns.

This Finnish space is shaped largely by the concept of *sisu*, a word that is notoriously difficult to translate. It means something like strength and grit, the ability to stick to something in the face of hardship, all while remaining calm and stoic. You'll see a bit of *sisu* in action when someone throws a little more water onto the stones of a sauna before finally jumping into the snow, or a nearby lake. You'll notice it in winter, when the temperature is -22°F (-30°C), and there are scores of Finns skiing and ice skating, enjoying everything that the coldest season has to offer. In fact, you'll see it all around you as you explore the modern

Finnish state, the result of two hard-fought wars for independence.

Finland isn't all grit and stoicism, however. It is, after all, the land of Alvar Aalto, the Finnish functionalist architect, of the composer Jean Sibelius, and of the myriad myths found within Elias Lönnrott's collected epic, the *Kalevala*. It's home to the films of Aki Kaurismäki, director, screenwriter, and auteur. And beyond music and literature, art and film, it is a thriving democracy. Low on crime, poverty, and corruption, it is no wonder that Finland is routinely found at the top of quality-of-life indexes. In other words, there is a great deal of beauty to be found beyond Finland's sprawling forests.

It is a stereotype that Finns are silent and reserved. While there is some truth to this, it isn't the whole story. If you spend some time here, if you break *ruisleipä* (rye bread) with them, and if you perhaps learn a word or two of Finnish, you'll learn that there's a lot more to be discovered: humor, fair-mindedness, resourcefulness, and generosity among them.

The winters are long and dark, so light a candle and you'll have something to see by. The summer days are endless, so don't go to sleep: stay up and watch a dusky sky turn to morning light. The language is notoriously difficult to learn, but not impossible: learn it and show yourself that a little *sisu* goes a long way. If you do these things, you will know more about what makes the Finns who they are—and, perhaps, find your own inner Finn.

Official Name	The Republic of Finland, *Suomen tasavalta*. Finland is *Suomi* in Finnish.	A member of the European Union and also of UN, IMF, GATT, WTO, World Bank, OECD, EEA, Nordic Council
Capital City	Helsinki (*Helsingfors*)	
Main Cities	Espoo, Tampere, Vantaa, Turku, Oulu, Lahti, Kuopio, Jyväskylä, and Pori	About 1,000,000 people live in the Helsinki metropolitan area.
Area	130,500 sq. miles (338,000 sq. km)	Slightly larger than the UK, Finland is the seventh-largest country in Europe.
Borders	Sweden, Norway, and Russia. Gulf of Finland and Gulf of Bothnia on the Baltic	
Climate	Northern European climate, with cold winters and warm summers	The Gulf Stream brings warmer weather from the Atlantic.
Currency	The Euro (EUR), divided into 100 cents	The Euro, introduced January 1, 2002, replaced the Finn Mark (Markka).
Population	5.5 million	65% live in urban areas, 35% in rural areas.
Ethnic Makeup	Majority are Finns, with small ethnic populations of Sami and Roma	
Other Nationalities	About 65,000 foreigners	Largest groups: Russians, Estonians, Ingrians

Family Makeup	Average household is 2.8 persons.	High divorce rate; aging population
Language	93% of Finns are Finnish-speaking, 5.6% speak Swedish. Both are official languages.	The Sami and Romany languages are also recognized.
Religion	Approx. 86% Lutheran; 1% Orthodox; 1% other	Approx. 12% do not belong to any religious group.
Government	Independent republic since December 6, 1917.	The head of state is the president, elected for a six-year term.
Media	Suomen Yleisradio (the Finnish Broadcasting Company) runs the main TV and radio channels. The main commercial TV channel is Mainostelevisio.	There are many commercial radio stations. The largest national newspaper is *Helsingin Sanomat*. Many national, regional, and local newspapers and magazines
Media: English Language	Much of the content found on Finnish TV is in English.	News summaries in English on web sites of major newspapers
Electricity	220/230 volts, 50 Hz	Two-prong plugs. Use transformers for US appliances.
Video/TV	Digital signal	
Internet Domain	.fi	
Telephone	The country code for Finland is +358.	
Time	2 hours ahead of Greenwich Mean Time; 7 hours ahead of Eastern Standard time	Daylight saving time (DST) from the last Sunday in March to the last Sunday in October

CHAPTER ONE

LAND & PEOPLE

GEOGRAPHICAL OVERVIEW

Finland is a land of lakes, forests, and open countryside. The Finns call their forests "green gold," as they provide the raw material for the paper and cellulose industries, both of which are major sources of wealth for the economy. Finland also leads in the international field of forestry research and sustainable development.

Most of the country is topographically low, with the highest hills located in Lapland. Eastern and southeastern Finland are characterized by a large number of lakes, while the west coast is very flat and prone to flooding. A glacier molded the countryside during the last Ice Age; you can see the large granite boulders that were left behind after the glacier melted.

The total area of Finland is 130,500 square miles (338,000 sq. km). The distance from the southernmost town of Hanko to the northernmost village of Nuorgam is measured at 719 miles (1,157 km), while the furthest distance east to west is a much narrower 336 miles (542 km). Finland is situated in the north of Europe between latitudes 60° and 70° and between longitudes 20° and 32°. he Arctic Circle runs through northern Finland, just north of Rovaniemi, and most of Lapland lies above it.

Finland shares a 381-mile (614-km) land border with Sweden to the west, and a 457-mile (736-km) border with Norway to the north. The eastern border

with Russia is the longest at 833 miles (1,340 km) and is patrolled by both Finnish and Russian border guards. This border marks the boundary of the European Union with the Russian Federal Republic and has been the backdrop for many spy novels set in the Cold War era. In the south, Finland borders on the Gulf of Finland and in the west the Gulf of Bothnia, both of which are part of the Baltic Sea. The length of the entire coastline is about 2,860 miles (4,600 km).

Water makes up around 10 percent of the total area of Finland. Forests, mainly pine and spruce,

cover 68 percent, and 6 percent of the land is under cultivation, with barley and oats as the main crops. The remaining terrain includes a great deal of marshy land. There are 187,888 lakes in total, so the name "land of a thousand lakes" is no myth, but rather an incredible understatement. Finland's 179,584 islands range from small skerries and outcrops to those with large inhabited towns. Nearly 100,000 of these islands are located in the lakes. Owning an island—or even several—is not unusual in Finland, and every Finn dreams of a house on a lake or by the sea.

Europe's largest archipelago lies off the southwest coast of Finland, and includes the Åland islands (Ahvenanmaa in Finnish), which are an autonomous province of Finland situated between Finland and Sweden. Their status as a demilitarized zone was decreed by the League of Nations in the 1920s. More than 90 percent of the population speak Swedish as their mother tongue.

The largest lake, Saimaa, is situated in southeast Finland. The main Finnish lakes form five long, navigable networks—in fact it is difficult to determine where one lake stops and another starts. There are still some car ferries in the more remote parts of the lakes, but bridges have replaced them in more densely populated areas. It is worth remembering that roads have to go around the largest lakes, making journeys long.

The numerous rivers provide hydroelectric power for the country. Salmon gates have been built on the traditional salmon migratory rivers. There are 5,100 rapids in Finland, the largest being at Imatra on the Russian border. These are now harnessed, but are sometimes released on a Sunday for the pleasure of tourists, and are a magnificent sight. From nearby Lappeenranta you can travel along the Saimaa Canal to Vyborg. If you want to do this trip, check with the tour company about whether or not you need a visa. The canal is leased to Finland by Russia, and runs through Russian Karelia to the Gulf of Finland, providing access from inland lake harbors to the oceans of the world. The city of Viipuri, which was the second-largest city in Finland before the Second World War, was ceded to Russia after the war.

CLIMATE

There are four distinct seasons in Finland, and they are startlingly different from one another. The longest season is winter, when frost and snow turn most of the countryside into a picture postcard. In Lapland the first snow can fall as early as September, and the winter does not come to an end until April or May. In the south the winter is much shorter and milder. Inland, the country is much colder and drier than the coastal areas. The temperatures in the north can fall as low as -40°F (-40°C). Lakes and coastal waters freeze in the winter, and the ice usually becomes thick enough to support traffic, which considerably shortens some journeys. The snow is at its thickest in March. Large quantities of snow are removed from the city centers to the outskirts for ski tracks and skating rinks. Icebreakers keep the main shipping routes open. The cost of the winter is huge to the Finnish economy.

Spring is dramatic, and can arrive suddenly, the ice on the lakes melting quickly. The summer can be very warm and dry, especially away from the coast, and daytime temperatures can rise to 86°F (30°C). Record temperatures are due to the continental weather coming in from the east. The west wind brings milder, wetter weather. Without the effect of the Gulf Stream, Finland would be a very cold and inhospitable country.

The Finns adore their short, precious summer, and enjoy every minute of it. Cafés spread out on to the streets, beer is consumed in large quantities on terraces, and sun worshipers fill the beaches. The gloriously colorful fall is a very popular time to go trekking in Lapland.

Because the lakes are shallow, the temperature of the water can be as warm as 68°F (20°C), making swimming in the summer a very pleasant experience. However, the Finns also swim in the lakes in winter—a hole is cut in the ice specially for them. This invigorating activity is said to cure many ills, and is certainly not for the faint-hearted! The annual world ice-swimming championships are held in Finland every winter.

The weather is very variable, and talking about the weather is something of a national pastime. Every household has an outdoor thermometer, because it is important to know how much or how little clothing you will need outside. Temperatures can change very quickly. Thunderstorms are common in the summer.

Days are short in the winter and long in the summer. In the north, the Polar night means that the sun doesn't rise at all for several weeks. In summer there is continuous daylight in Lapland for about two months. Even in the south the sun only sets for a short while in midsummer. The magnificent light show of the aurora borealis, or the northern lights (the Finns call them "fox fire"), can

be seen on clear, dark nights, on average three out of four nights. The best and most frequent views are from the Kilpisjärvi region, in Lapland, but the lights can sometimes be seen in the south of the country as well.

WILDLIFE

The abundance of water and the warmer weather bring the curse of the Finnish summer: the mosquitoes. These irritating creatures are not so common in towns, but are all the more voracious near lakes and marshes and in the forests, and are particularly plentiful in Lapland. Although these mosquitoes do not carry any diseases, some people have a severe reaction to their bites. If this is the case, seek advice from a pharmacist, who will recommend repellents and ointments. Some Finns swear that beer is the best repellent, but you have to drink large quantities for it to be effective! World mosquito-killing championships are held every summer, the winner being the one who kills the most, using hands only, in a given time. Finns are well practiced at this sport.

There are no polar bears in Finland, contrary to statements made in some guidebooks, but there are brown bears. Most of these are in eastern Finland, but there have been sightings as far south as the outskirts of Helsinki. They present no danger to humans, but can be very bold when they have cubs, and hungry bears are known to kill domestic animals. The ancient Finns worshiped the bear as the king of the forest, and Finnish has more than fifty words for bear—it was believed that you had to refer to it by euphemisms; otherwise the bear thought it was being called, and that was the last thing anyone wanted. Recently, a bear

on the runway at Joensuu airport held up domestic flights.

Finns also worshiped the elk, or moose. Some of the earliest cave paintings depict elks, and some of the earliest decorative objects are in the shape of an elk's head. The modern Finns hunt elk. A foreigner wishing to hunt in Finland will need to pass a hunter's test and have the appropriate permit and a Finnish guide. All elk hunters have to wear red or orange hats to avoid shooting each other! The number of permits varies according to the elk population. These large animals are a major hazard on the roads, as are reindeer in Lapland.

There are also many wolves, again predominantly in eastern and northern Finland, but frequent sightings occur all over the country. The rarest mammal is the Saimaa seal, found in the waters near Savonlinna and Linnansaari. Wildfowl include ptarmigan and grouse, and bird migration to the Arctic regions provides bird-watchers with plenty to see in the spring and fall. The ornithologists' paradise is Hangonniemi, the southernmost point of Finland, where the birds rest after crossing the Baltic Sea. The migration of the swans is said to have inspired the first symphony of Sibelius.

The Finnish lakes and coastal waters teem with fish. Pike, perch, and pikeperch are some of the most commonly caught freshwater fish, together with different species of salmon, including the vendace, which is caught by trawling.

A BRIEF HISTORY

From Ice Age to Iron Age

Who are the Finns, and where did they come from? Finns were first mentioned by the historian Tacitus in his history of Germany, but there is very little written evidence about them before the Romans occupied the area. It is known that Finnish hunters traded furs with the Germans, who sold them to the Romans.

The migration of Finnic peoples can be traced through linguistic loans and similarities with other peoples around the eastern Baltic, along the Volga River in Russia, and all the way to the areas around the Ural Mountains, where languages related to

Finnish are still spoken. There are many peoples, including the Estonians, the Ingrians, the Votyaks, and others, who share a linguistic past with the Finns. With modern DNA analysis it has been established that the Finns share around 75 percent of their genes with the Europeans of the Baltic region, and only about 25 percent of the genes come from the East or are of Asian origin. The Hungarian language is also remotely related to Finnish.

There are still many unanswered questions about the Finns and the Sami people. Did the Sami people, who now speak a language related to Finnish, speak some other language before? Who were the Battle-Axe people, and what language did they speak?

Archaeological finds would indicate that the first people—probably hunter-gatherers—arrived in Finland around 8000 BCE, some time after the end of the last Ice Age. We don't know who these people were, or what language they spoke. The area may have been populated before then, but the glacier would have destroyed any evidence. New finds are being made, and historians may have to reassess the prehistory of the area.

The Finns moved to the area that is now Finland from the south, across the Gulf of Finland, and from the east, along the Karelian Isthmus. There was also some migration from the east coast of Sweden to the coastal areas of western and southwestern Finland along the gulf of Bothnia. The Åland Islands were also inhabited very early. All these areas are still predominantly Swedish-speaking.

There have been some very interesting prehistoric finds in Finland, including some spectacular cave and rock paintings. In addition to the archaeological finds, there are the tales of the *Kalevala*, which tell the story of the heroes of the North fighting battles and carrying out feats of power and intelligence.

The pagan Finns had their own gods. The chief god, Ukko, remains in the language as the word for thunder. Many place-names refer to sacrificial grounds and burial places. Modern methods of research and scientific analysis are constantly revealing more about the past.

The Vikings traveled through Finland on their long journeys to the East. The ancient trading routes still exist, mainly the Kuninkaantie, the King's route, which passes through southern Finland from Stockholm via Turku and on to Russia. Parts of this are a heritage trail today.

From First Crusade to Grand Duchy

More is known about Finland after the Northern Crusades reached the country. Christianity probably arrived in Sweden with Irish monks. The first crusade to Finland took place in 1155, according to legends dating from the end of the thirteenth century, led by St. Henry, the bishop of Uppsala, and King Eric of Sweden.

Papal power was extending its reach from the west; meanwhile the Orthodox faith was actively converting from the east. Sweden wanted to secure the area of Finland, not just for the Catholic Church, but also politically as its frontier toward the east. Ever since then, Finland has been between these two interest

Saint Henry baptizes the Finns at the spring of Kuppis, close to Turku. Painting by R.W. Ekman, 1854.

groups. The western Finns aligned with the Catholic Church, and the Karelians in the east with the Orthodox faith prevalent in Novgorod, the predecessor to the state of Russia.

The emerging Swedish state tied Finland closer to itself, the first documentary evidence regarding Finland as a part of Sweden appearing in a papal document in 1216. Sweden built fortifications in Häme, Vyborg, and on the south coast. Vyborg Castle, built in 1293, still stands, and is now in Russia. Castles were also built in Turku and Savonlinna, both of which still stand.

In 1323, under the Treaty of Pähkinänsaari, Sweden and Novgorod divided Finland between the two kingdoms. Karelia came under Novgorod rule, and the west and south of Finland remained within Western culture and the Catholic Church as a part of the Swedish state.

Turku became the capital of the Swedish province of Finland. The Swedish legal system, taxation, and other tools of the state were established. The bishop of Turku became the spiritual leader of the country. Finns had a right to send representatives to the Diet in Sweden in the sixteenth century.

The Reformation and the Lutheran Protestant Church were established in Finland, as elsewhere in Scandinavia, in the first half of the sixteenth century. As Sweden's power grew and expanded eastward, Finland increasingly became a battleground, and hunger and wars taxed the population. Swedish controls were tightened, and Swedes held all the high offices of state.

The glory of the Swedish empire came to an end in the Great Northern War (1700–21). Russia occupied Finland in 1714, when Swedish attention was elsewhere. Then followed the so-called period of the Great Wrath, ending in the Peace of Uusikaupunki in 1721, and southeast Finland became part of Russia. Further battles followed, and Russia's sphere of influence pushed ever further west. There were some fledgling feelings for a Finnish state at this time, and some talk of separating Finland from Sweden. The university in Turku was the center of intellectual activity, but there was still a long way to go before Finland was ready to be a nation-state.

During the reign of Sweden's King Gustavus III (1771–92), there were some improvements in Finland. Work started on the fortification of Viaborg, just outside Helsinki, now known as Suomenlinna. This fort has been attacked only once—by the British during the Crimean War.

This was a period of renaissance for Finland, with improvements in government and the economy, and new towns founded. Some of the officers involved in the war against Russia (1788–90) advocated separation from Sweden, but received little support for their ideas.

In the meantime, Napoleon Bonaparte was enlarging his empire in Europe. In 1807 he met Alexander I of Russia in Tilsit, in Poland. They agreed that Sweden should be coerced to join the French blockade against Great Britain, and to force Sweden's hand Russia attacked Finland. This war (1808–9) is known as the War of Finland. The fictional description of the war by Johan Ludvig Runeberg in his narrative poem "The stories of Ensign Ståhl" inspired the Finnish romantic movement, which in turn fueled the nationalist movement of the nineteenth century. The Russians defeated the Swedes, and occupied Finland.

Tsar Alexander I was eager to secure the defenses of St. Petersburg, and it was important to have Finland as part of Russia. After the peace was agreed to in 1809, Alexander I came to Finland and opened the first session of the Finnish Diet in Porvoo. The Finns swore allegiance to Russia, and in return were allowed to keep

Russian Tsar Alexander I.

their Lutheran faith, constitutional laws, and rights established during the Swedish reign. Finland became part of Russia as an autonomous Grand Duchy. Alexander I was a constitutional monarch, and his representative in Finland was a governor-general. The Finnish Senate was established with a four-estate Diet. For the first time, Finland had the machinery of a state. The Tsar favored a strong Finland to weaken Sweden further.

Helsinki became the capital of Finland, and grew rapidly. Viipuri, which had been established as a trading town during the Hanseatic League, flourished, and became the most cosmopolitan town of the Grand Duchy. It was said that many of the citizens of Viipuri were fluent in four languages— Russian, German, Swedish, and Finnish.

From Grand Duchy to Independence

There was growing interest in establishing a Finnish identity. Elias Lönnrot gathered and recorded in writing the oral traditions of poetry and mythical tales of Finnish heroes, which later became, under his editorship, the *Kalevala*. The publication of these epic verses added to the nascent pride in the Finnish language. The subject of language went through bitter disagreements, throughout the eighteenth century and into the nineteenth, between the supporters of Swedish and those of Finnish. This language issue still has echoes in today's Finland. Fueled by Runeberg's patriotic poetry and by the philosophy and practical

achievements of Senator Johan Vilhelm Snellman, the
first Finnish-language schools were established in the
1860s. Finnish was also established in the university
system as a teaching language. This in itself led to great
innovation and work on the language. Words like *tiede*
(science) and *taide* (art) were coined by the innovators
of literary Finnish, the liberal attitude of Tsar Alexander
II making these advances possible.

The Pan-Slavist movement under Tsars Alexander
III and Nikolai II led to measures to diminish the
rights of the Finns. Political freedoms were lost, but
arts and literature flourished. The Golden Age of
Finnish Art received international acclaim at the Paris
World Exhibition of 1900, where Finns had their own
pavilion for the first time. The composer Sibelius had
become world famous, and his *Finlandia* the anthem
of Finnish nationalists.

The turning point in the Russo–Finnish relationship
came after Russia suffered heavy losses in the Russo–
Japanese War. The unrest in Russia spread to Finland,
and the Finnish Diet went through a radical reform.
The four estates were replaced by a unicameral
parliament, and universal suffrage was established,
Finnish women being the first women in Europe to
be granted the right to vote.

The Civil War

In the first decade of the twentieth century the Russian
grip tightened further, and Finnish autonomy was
severely restricted. In Finland, Russians were given

equal rights with Finns by law, and political activity was closely monitored by the Russian authorities. Among many Finnish activists, the senator P. E. Svinhufvud was sent to Siberia. He later became president of Finland. The First World War and internal political turmoil in Russia culminated in the Russian Revolution in 1917 and the end of the power of the Tsars. In Finland the senate under the leadership of Svinhufvud made a declaration of independence on December 6, 1917. The Soviet government, led by Lenin, recognized Finland's new independence a month later.

A bitter civil war followed in Finland. The opposing forces of the left, known as the Reds (landless rural workers and factory workers), and the right, the Whites (the aristocracy, army, and bourgeoisie), some of whom had been trained as the Jaeger battalion in Germany, fought a bitter war that left deep divisions in Finland for a long time. The Whites, led by Carl Gustav Emil Mannerheim, defeated their opponents, and a victory march was organized in Helsinki in May 1918. Mannerheim became the temporary head of state. There were some moves to establish a monarchy in Finland, but under the new constitution Finland became a republic. In 1919 K. J. Ståhlberg was elected the first president. In the same year alcohol was prohibited, and this prohibition lasted until 1932. In 1921, certain tenant workers gained the right to buy their land.

By this time Finnish culture had been further established by the continued success of Finnish arts and literature. Finns were successful at the Stockholm

Olympics, with Hannes Kolehmainen winning three
gold medals in running. The Finnish-language weekly
Suomen Kuvalehti was founded, and the news agency
Suomen Tietotoimisto was established.

Between the Wars

In the 1920s the young republic started to establish
its institutions. Education was made compulsory, and
both Finnish and Swedish became official languages.
National Service was started in 1922. Right-wing
tendencies grew, leading to conflict with the left-
wing parties, and many arrests of prominent socialist
politicians followed. The right-wing Lapuan Liike
movement was established in 1929.

The 1920s brought light entertainment, ranging from
cinema to jazz and tango, into the country. Gramophone
records sold in large numbers and the Finnish
Broadcasting Company, Yleisradio, was set up. Women
were allowed to join the civil service. Commercial
aviation started. At the end of the decade, Finland
plunged into depression following the Wall Street crash.

The 1930s saw more antisocialist measures. The
right-wing "blackshirts" kidnapped the president; the
unrest culminated in the so-called Mäntsälä rebellion
in 1932, after which the right-wing activity was
curtailed but not eradicated.

The Finnish film industry went from strength to
strength. Architecture saw the seminal work of Alvar
Aalto in the Viipuri Library, finished in 1935. Some of
the rifts caused by the civil war were starting to mend.

The growth of the power of Germany and the looming possibility of war cast a shadow on the general air of optimism that had spread in Finland. In 1939 Frans Emil Sillanpää won the Nobel Prize for Literature, and the summer Olympics were due to be staged in Finland in 1940. The Olympic stadium was completed.

The Winter War

Russians wanted to establish military bases on some of the islands in the Gulf of Finland to protect Leningrad. Negotiations were long and unsuccessful. Russia attacked Finland on November 30, 1939. The short, bitter war finished on March 13, 1940. The winter was exceptionally cold, and the losses were heavy. Karelia was lost to Russia, and the Karelians were all evacuated to Finland. The peace was short-lived and the so-called Continuation War started on June 25, 1940. A truce was declared in September 1944.

Early in the Second World War, the German forces occupying Norway crossed over to Lapland in an attempt to sever Allied supply lines to Leningrad. In 1944–5, the German troops still in Lapland retreated, devastating and burning most of the country, including the capital, Rovaniemi. The Paris Peace Treaty of 1947 ordered Finland to pay heavy war reparations to the Soviet Union and to cede the Karelian Isthmus and part of Lapland to the Soviet Union. The Karelian refugees were housed all around Finland. Rationing continued until the 1950s. The return of the soldiers from the front resulted in the biggest baby boom in Finnish history in the years 1945 to 1950.

Postwar Finland

In 1948 the Treaty of Friendship, Cooperation and Mutual Assistance was concluded with the Soviet Union, and was discontinued only in the early 1990s, when the Soviet Union disintegrated. President Paasikivi established the so-called Paasikivi Line, which continued with his successor Urho Kekkonen. The reparations had forced the Finnish economy to undergo a regeneration and radical change. The Olympics of 1952, held in Helsinki, established Finland on the international map, and to top the success of the year the legendary Finnish beauty Armi Kuusela was crowned Miss Universe.

Finland joined the United Nations in 1955. In the same year the Nordic Council with Sweden, Denmark, and Norway was established, creating a free-trade area. In foreign policy the line of neutrality and nonalignment was actively promoted by President Kekkonen. Finland joined EFTA as an associate member and signed a free-trade agreement with the EEC.

Coca-Cola and rock and roll arrived toward the end of the 1950s. Finnish design came into world prominence with names like Tapio Wirkkala, Kaj Franck, Timo Sarpaneva, and Antti Nurmesniemi. Marimekko was founded by Armi Ratia. Alvar Aalto was a world leader in architecture. *The Unknown Soldier*, a pacifist novel about the war by Väinö Linna, became a huge success, and was made into a film that broke all box-office records.

Politically, the start of the 1960s saw a chilling of Finno–Soviet relations, culminating in the Note Crisis of 1961 over the nomination of one of the candidates for the presidential elections. President Kekkonen continued in office through the whole decade. The Finnish economy grew. There was monetary reform, one new mark replacing one hundred old marks. Forestry and the paper industry, together with shipbuilding and the metal industry, flourished. The baby boomers were squeezed out of the country to the cities, and Helsinki continued to grow. Finland grew closer and closer to the rest of Europe.

Culturally, the decade was marked by the blasphemy case against the novelist Hannu Salama and his description of Jesus in *Juhannustanssit*; the book was banned. A second television channel, TV2, started in Tampere; "Let's Kiss," the Finnish dance, made the world pop charts; and the Beatles and Elvis competed in popular music charts with Finnish tango. Left-wing radicalism was popular among students and artists. One of the main events of the decade was the staging of *Lapualaisooppera*, the musical retelling of the fascist movement of the 1930s. The University of Tampere, which became the leading university for media and social studies, was founded. The Pori Jazz Festival and the Kaustinen Folk Music Festival were started. There was a change of generations in architecture with Dipoli completed by the Pietilä husband and wife team. The comprehensive school system was adopted. The 1968 French students' revolt reached Finland with the occupation of the Student Union House in Helsinki. The liberalization of attitudes also resulted in mid-strength beer becoming available from supermarkets and shops. Finns took to bingo, and started to travel to the Mediterranean sun on package tours. Even the language changed, with the use of the informal address, *sinuttelu*, replacing the formal, *teitittely*.

The economy moved into recession by the mid 1970s due to the global oil crisis, and migration to the cities and to Sweden continued. Finland became established in the international arena as a nonaligned, politically neutral state, though there were accusations, particularly from Germany, that Finland was under the control of the Soviet Union. "Finlandization," as a term, came into existence. The OECD conference was held in Finland, finishing with the signing of the Helsinki agreement. In internal politics, the period was marked by the birth of many protest parties. The biggest of these was the SMP, or *S*uomen Maaseudun Puolue, led by Veikko Vennamo.

The national lottery came into being, and Lasse Viren won gold medals in the Munich Olympics. The first-ever rock festivals were held in Turku. The Savonlinna Opera Festival was revived by Martti Talvela. New Finnish operas were composed by Joonas Kokkonen and Aulis Sallinen.

The economy continued to grow, and went through the heady yuppie years. The Metro was built in Helsinki. Environmental issues came to the forefront, the Ministry of Environment was set up, and the Green movement became a political party. The mutual aid agreement with the Soviet Union was extended by twenty years in 1985, but it was annulled in 1992 following the collapse of the Soviet Union. Women could be ordained, but only after a long debate in the Church. Equal rights legislation came into force and a new law on surnames made it possible for women to keep their surname on marriage. Many women went back to using their maiden names, or combined their maiden and married names. The state monopoly on broadcasting came to an end, and the first commercial radio stations started up. The long-term president Urho Kekkonen died in 1986, marking the end of the postwar years.

The 1990s witnessed the economic crisis precipitated by the fall of the Soviet Union and the end of oil barter trade. A banking crisis followed in Finland, and the state had to intervene to safeguard the savings banks. Unemployment reached record levels. Finland applied to join the European Union, and a referendum was held in 1994 with 56.9 percent of Finns voting for joining and 43.1 percent voting against. The split between urban and rural Finland was marked, with urban Finland voting "yes," and rural areas voting "no."

The national highlight of the decade was in May 1995, when Finland won the world ice hockey championships in Stockholm. The Finnish telecommunications company Nokia led the whole world in mobile telephone technology. The Finnish economy grew very fast. Moving into the twenty-first century, Finland is becoming very well established in the European Union. There is continuing debate in Finland about the pros and cons of joining NATO.

GOVERNMENT AND POLITICS

Finland is a sovereign parliamentary republic. The original constitution came into force in July 1919, and there were no major changes until the year 2000. The constitution lays down the rules for the highest organs of the state and the constitutional rights of its citizens. The ultimate power is vested in the people, who elect 200 representatives to the Finnish parliament. These elections take place in March every four years, and the electoral system is direct and proportional. The parliament traditionally has representatives of many parties.

Finland has a strong tradition of coalition governments and consensus politics. The welfare state is on the agenda of all Finnish political parties, although there has been a push toward cuts to these programs in recent years. Women are strongly represented in the

Parliament House, the seat of Finnish government, Helsinki.

Finnish government. Since 2000, approximately half of all government ministers have been female. The prime minister is selected by the parliament in an open vote according to the revised constitution of March 2000.

The presidential elections are held every six years. The maximum period for one president is two consecutive terms of office. Tarja Halonen became the first female president in March 2000. The current president, Sauli Niinistö, will hold the position until 2024 after winning reelection in 2018.

The president, together with the government, forms the Council of State. The prime minister proposes the ministerial posts, and the president officially appoints the cabinet of at least twelve, but no more than eighteen, ministers. The council of state has executive power and the parliament legislative power.

Local government elections are held every four years in the fall. Each municipal authority has a local council with extensive powers, including local taxation, hospitals, health centers, town planning, welfare, and education. The state assists local authorities from central funds. Finland has 446 local authorities, 111 of which are towns. There are plans to merge local authorities to form larger administrative areas. Regional government is divided into five regions, led by the regional governor. Åland has its own local autonomous government.

Foreign policy is led by the parliament and the president. The duties of representing Finland in international affairs are divided between the president and the prime minister under the amended constitution.

In 1999 Finnish voters elected sixteen representatives into the European Parliament for a five-year term. Finnish is an official language in the European Union. Finnish MEPs included Ari Vatanen, the 1981 world motor-rally driving champion, and Marjo Matikainen-Kallström, a many times cross-country skiing world champion. It is not unusual for sportsmen and pop stars to go into politics in Finland. Antti Kalliomäki, the Minister for Finance, is a champion pole-vaulter, Lasse Viren, the four-times Olympic gold medalist, is a member of parliament. The Minister for Culture, Tanja Karpela, was a Miss Finland.

Finns have traditionally been very active voters, but young Finns today are less interested in politics than in single-issue movements and environmental organizations. There is also an increasing number of small splinter parties, for instance parties representing old-age pensioners.

FINLAND AND ITS NEIGHBORS

Until the early nineteenth century, Finland's role in history was to be the battleground for supremacy between Sweden and Russia. Since its independence in 1917, Finland has clashed with the Soviet Union, but has had a peaceful coexistence with Sweden.

Estonia is regarded as a special neighbor by Finns, because of their linguistic and cultural similarities. Even though Finland shares a border with Norway, the remoteness of the border area means that there is much less contact with the Norwegians. The Sami people inhabit the area of northern Finnish Lapland, northern Norway, Sweden, and Russia, and have a Sami Council, which promotes their affairs across the whole area.

There is a love–hate relationship between the Finns and the Swedes. Finns like to tell jokes about the Swedes and the Russians. Seven hundred years of providing soldiers for the Swedish army, and of paying the Swedes heavy taxes to run the administration, left their mark. The lean years of the Finnish economy forced large numbers of Finns to move to Sweden to work. Finns were regarded as second-class citizens in the early years of this migration, but now that Sweden has large numbers of immigrants Finns are more highly regarded, and their children have integrated into Swedish society.

Sports matches between the two nations are always bitterly fought. The Finns and the Swedes get along well, though there are sometimes problems when commercial companies merge—the Swedes like a wide consultation process, while the Finns want quick decisions.

The relationship with Russia and formerly with the Soviet Union is complex. Since the breakup of the Soviet Union travel has become easier. The Orthodox monastery of Valamo in Lake Ladoga is a very popular tourist destination for Finns. There are a number of collaborative projects, including the restoration of the library in Viipuri, which is one of the early works of the Finnish functionalist architect Alvar Aalto.

Many Karelian Finns, who lost their homes in the Second World War, vehemently hate the Russians, and dream of having Karelia back. Large numbers of Karelians and many war veterans travel frequently to see their homeland or battlefields in Karelia.

Finns are starting to analyze the Soviet years more objectively, but there is still a long way to go. Many memoirs and diaries, and the opening up of the Kremlin archives, are providing rich material for historians. There is no doubt that the 1950s, '60s, and '70s were a difficult time. Economically the Soviet Union was for Finland a huge and eager consumer market as well as a buyer of industrial machinery. The breakup of the Soviet Union plunged the Finnish economy into a downward spiral, from which it has now fully recovered. Finnish companies are once again expanding into Russian markets. On the political front, the so-called Northern Dimension, or Finland's strategic position as a gateway from the EU to Russia, is much discussed.

THE FINNS TODAY

There are approximately 5.5 million people living in Finland today, nearly 80 percent of whom are concentrated in urban areas. This is in stark contrast to only a century earlier, when 90 percent lived of people lived in rural areas and were engaged in agriculture. The social and economic changes as a result of urban migration have been enormous.

The average life expectancy of a Finn is eighty-two years. The demographic pyramid resembles that of most other industrial countries, with the middle-aged group predominating. The "baby boomers" of the postwar years are nearing or have entered retirement age. Nearly 86 percent of Finns belong to the Lutheran Church, and just over 1 percent to the Finnish Orthodox Church.

Finland also has a Sami population of 6,500, who speak several different dialects of the Sami language, and who traditionally herd reindeer. There are also Sami people living in northern Norway, Sweden, and Russia. Tourism is now a very important source of income. Winter tourism to Lapland has increased with trips to visit Santa Claus, who lives there, according to the Finns! Lapland is also growing in popularity as a destination for skiing and trekking.

The profile of the Sami people has been significantly raised in the last couple of decades with the Sami Parliament and the University of Lapland. Sami culture has gained in popularity, with such artists as Wimme and the folk group Angelin Tytöt singing modern versions of a traditional Sami singing style, *joiku*. There is also a newly found fascination with shamanism. There is an outstanding issue between the reindeer-herding Sami people and the Finnish state over landowning rights.

Only about 243,600 foreigners live in Finland, many of whom are refugees. Most foreigners have moved to Finland to work, to study, or to marry a Finn. The largest group of those with foreign backgrounds living in Finland are Estonians, followed by Russians, Iraqis, and Chinese. The refugee and migrant crisis, which began in 2015, has also had an impact. By international comparison the numbers are small, but the homogeneous Finland of old is slowly moving toward multiculturalism. The influx of new people, the increase in numbers of Finns working abroad, and the general trend of globalization are all having an effect on the Finns and Finnish culture.

Agriculture, forestry, and the construction industry provide a livelihood for a significant portion of the Finnish population, as do the electronics, paper, and energy industries. The paper industry, once Finland's largest economic contributor, has shrunk considerably. Likewise, the pervasiveness of the electronics industry has diminished, with Nokia's loss of its share of the cell phone market.

The recession of the early 1990s started to drive a wedge between the well-to-do and those in danger of social exclusion, including the long-term unemployed. Life was good in the heady days of the 1980s welfare state, but the cost was too high. A banking crisis and the worsening economy brought about redundancies and cutbacks in public spending. Elderly people, young families, and those in sparsely populated rural areas are among those most likely to suffer economic hardship, and there are regular soup kitchens in some deprived urban areas. Life continues to be very good for those who are employed.

FINNISH THINGS YOU MAY BE FAMILIAR WITH

Finland is a small, relatively new country, but it is known internationally for quite a few things:

- **Nokia**: Many people all over the world remember their first cell phone, and there is a good chance that that phone was a Nokia. The company experienced an enormous blow with the release of the iPhone and the rise of smartphones, but it is still around, still producing phones, tablets, tires, and rubber boots.

- **Linux**: Created by a Finn by the name of Linus Torvalds, Linux is a free and open-source computer operating system.

- **Sauna**: The only internationally recognized Finnish loanword.

- **Finnish education**: One of the things Finland is most famous for is its stellar education system. People from all over the world come to behold Finnish schools and to see what they're doing differently.

- **Finlandia**: Whether the vodka brand or the soaring anthem by Jean Sibelius, you have probably heard the term "Finlandia" at some point in your life. The vodka, globally renowned, is produced using Finnish-grown barley and glacial spring water.

CITIES IN FINLAND

Helsinki

Helsinki, capital of Finland and "the daughter of the Baltic," is a scenic seaside town, situated on the south coast, on the shores of the Gulf of Finland. It was known in the rest of the world by its Swedish name, Helsingfors, right up to the Second World War. The airport is 12 miles (20 km) from the city center.

Helsinki is a lively modern city and the largest in Finland with more than 650,000 inhabitants. The surrounding capital region, which includes the

Helsinki Cathedral overlooking the harbor of central neighborhood of Kruununhaka.

Townhouses built around a common courtyard make up many of Helsinki's residential neighborhoods.

smaller cities of Vantaa, Espoo, and Kauniainen, is home to over 1.2 million people, more than 20 percent of the country's population. There are many beautiful islands. The warm summers provide a perfect setting for outdoor activities, but in the bitterly cold winters, with icy winds from the open sea, people stay indoors. The Havis Amanda statue by Ville Vallgren is the symbol of the town and the focal point of many festivities.

Helsinki was founded in 1550 by the King of Sweden, Gustav Wasa. For a couple of centuries it remained an insignificant town, almost dying out at one time, but the annexation of Finland by Russia saw the start of rapid growth and development. The Russian authorities wanted a capital closer to St. Petersburg, and in 1812 Helsinki became the new capital. The old capital,

Turku, suffered a disastrous fire in 1827, after which
the university was moved to Helsinki. The university
is the largest in the country. There had also been a fire
in Helsinki a few years before it became the capital,
and this spurred the rebuilding of the town, in the
neoclassical style, designed by Carl Ludvig Engel. The
oldest part of Helsinki is the Suomenlinna fortress,
built on a group of islands fifteen minutes by boat
from the south harbor. Helsinki grew rapidly through
the nineteenth century to become the largest city in
Finland, and the twentieth-century migration from
the countryside has made Helsinki and the towns
surrounding it home for one in five Finns.

The architecture of Helsinki is a mixture of the
neoclassical center, the Finnish national romantic
style, and modern and postmodernist architecture.
One of the latest landmarks is the modern art museum,
Kiasma. The Olympic Stadium was built at the end
of the 1930s, but, because of the Second World War,
the Olympics were not held in Helsinki until 1952.
Helsinki is a great ice hockey town, with the new Ice
Stadium and the Hartwall Arena. All three venues are
also used for pop concerts.

Helsinki has a permanent amusement park,
Linnanmäki (open during the summer months only).
Korkeasaari Island houses the town's zoological
gardens. Seurasaari Island is the home for a large
collection of traditional Finnish wooden buildings and
lots of red squirrels! In fact, for anybody interested in
modern architecture there is a great deal to see. You

will find guidebooks and brochures at the Helsinki City Tourist Office in the beautiful Jugendstil building not far from the famous market in the south harbor.

The church in Temppelinaukio, "the rock church," is another famous landmark, together with Alvar Aalto's last building, the Finlandia Hall, where the Conference for Security and Co-operation in Europe was held in 1975. This conference put Helsinki firmly on the international map, with the Helsinki Agreement bringing East and West closer to each other.

Helsinki has a large number of interesting museums and other places to visit. You might start by taking the number 3T tram, which takes you around the main sights.

The rock church at Temppelinaukio, situated in Helsinki's Töölö neighborhood.

The Kiasma Museum of Modern Art, one of the city's many cultural offerings.

For the artistically and culturally inclined, there is a lot on offer. Some of the best Finnish art is in the national museum of Ateneum and in the many private collections that are open to the public; there are also, of course, commercial art galleries. Clubbing and eating out are excellent, and there are many annual festivals and sporting events. Check the local press for details.

It is convenient to buy a "Helsinki card" when you want to get around the town and see the sights. It comes with a guidebook, and entitles you not only to free travel on public transportation (buses, metro, trains, boats) but also to free entry to all the main tourist attractions and approximately fifty museums. It will also get you reductions on sight-seeing tours, the Finnair airport bus, car rentals, restaurants, cafés, shopping, and various sports and saunas. The card is valid for one, two, or three days. You can travel from Helsinki by boat to Stockholm and Tallinn as well as to Poland and Germany and by train to Russia.

Espoo

This is the second-largest city in Finland, with about 220,000 inhabitants. Situated on the south coast, just to the west of Helsinki, Espoo has a beautiful coastline and much unspoiled natural beauty, including the Nuuksio National Park. The famous King's Road, which connects Stockholm with Finland and Russia, runs through the town.

There is a long history to Espoo, which has its roots in prehistoric settlements from as early as 3500 BCE. The parish church dates from the fifteenth century. Espoo has as one of its centers the Tapiola garden city, which is a model for town planning for architects the world over. Today Tapiola is a leading technology center in northern Europe.

The Helsinki University of Technology is in Otaniemi, near Tapiola. The former student union building, Dipoli, is a masterpiece by Reima Pietilä and Raili Paatelainen. The campus and university buildings are by Alvar Aalto.

The organic architecture of the Dipoli building, today the main building of Aalto University, uses native Finnish materials such as pine wood, copper, and natural rock.

Vantaa

Vantaa, situated due north of Helsinki, is most famous as the location of the Helsinki-Vantaa Airport, which has several times been voted the best airport in the world. Many leading high-tech and logistics companies are situated around it. The Finnish science center Heureka is in Tikkurila. Ainola, the museum home of the great Finnish composer Jean Sibelius, is on Lake Tuusulanjärvi.

Close to it is another interesting museum—the studio
and home of the famous Finnish painter Pekka
Halonen, of the Golden Age of Finnish art. There was
a very lively bohemian artistic population around the
lake at the turn of the twentieth century.

Tampere

Tampere, 109 miles (175 km) north of Helsinki, is
situated in the region of Häme, on the banks of the
Tammerkoski rapids, which run between two large lakes.
Founded by the Swedish King Gustav III in 1779, the
town is called Tammerfors in Swedish. It was a center for
the textile industry, and was one of the birthplaces of the
trade union movement in Finland. During the Finnish
Civil War one of the fiercest battles was fought here.
Tampere is now the biggest inland town in the Nordic
countries, and the second-largest regional center in
Finland after the Greater Helsinki area.

Tampere has two universities, and has produced
some of the most famous names in Finnish media and
journalism. It is also well known as a theater town.
The cathedral was designed by Lars Sonck, and its
murals are by the Finnish symbolist painter Hugo
Simberg. Modern art is well represented in the Sara
Hilden Art Museum. The city's main library, in the
shape of an owl, is by Raili and Reima Pietilä. Lenin,
the Russian leader, stayed in Tampere during his exile,
and there is a museum dedicated to him. Särkänniemi
Adventure Park is the most popular amusement park
in Finland.

Turku's once Catholic cathedral is today the Mother Church of the Evangelical Lutheran Church of Finland.

Turku

Turku (Åbo in Swedish) is the oldest city in Finland, the former capital under Swedish rule, and the regional center of southwestern Finland. It is situated on the banks of the Aura River, close to the Turku archipelago, and is surrounded by beautiful countryside. The "Christmas city" of Finland, Turku hosts the special declaration of Christmas peace on December 24 and many events between November and January. In the summer the rock festival of Ruissalo brings crowds of young people to the town.

Turku has two universities, two schools of economics—one Swedish-speaking and one Finnish-speaking—and many high-tech companies. Traditionally the gateway to the west, the harbor is busy and important. Turku has always been a major commercial center, and its name, in fact, means "market place." It has suffered many devastating fires during its long history. The castle, parts of which date from the twelfth century, and the medieval cathedral are the main sights, but there is also the handicrafts museum in the Luostarinmäki, the only

street that survived the great fire of 1827. The tall ship *Suomen Joutsen* is anchored on the river, and is now a museum. There are many art galleries and museums, one of the most interesting being the combination of old and new in the Aboa Vetus and Ars Nova complex.

Oulu

Oulu, in the north, is another important regional town. It is now a leading high-tech center with a thriving university, but its history as the most important tar port in Europe goes back four hundred years. It is the fastest-growing urban center outside the Greater Helsinki area. It is often referred to as Finland's Silicon Valley; its technology village, Technopolis, was founded in 1982.

Rovaniemi

Further north, in Lapland, is the town of Rovaniemi. Burned down by the Germans at the end of the Second World War, it has now been completely rebuilt. The Christmas charter flights, bringing tourists to see Santa Claus, land here.

Lahti

In the south of Finland the city of Lahti has become an important conference center with its new Sibelius Hall, the largest wooden building built in Finland for a hundred years and, surprisingly, the first concert hall to bear the name of Sibelius. The hall is home to the Lahti Symphony Orchestra, led by Osmo Vänskä, who has become a leading interpreter of Sibelius's music. Lahti is also an important winter sports center, with two huge ski jumps, and is the starting point for the 100-kilometer Finlandia ski event every winter.

Lappeenranta

If you are interested in experiencing Finnish nature, yet do not want to stray too far from Helsinki, Lappeenranta is the city for you. A two-hour train ride from the capital, the city is situated on the shores of Lake Saimaa, the largest lake in Finland. Lappeenranta's historical fortress contains Finland's oldest Russian Orthodox church, two museums, and several cafés, and is located high on a hill, overlooking the city, the harbor, and the expansive lake. It is well worth a visit. At the harbor you can hop on a cruise ship and explore the surrounding area, or even take a three-day cruise to St. Petersburg, Russia. The cruises to Russia are visa-free.

If you are traveling in summertime, and particularly if you are traveling with children, you may enjoy visiting Lappeenranta's famous sandcastle. Every summer, the city of Lappeenranta commissions artists from around the world to design and build a new giant sandcastle, something it has been doing since 2003.

CHAPTER TWO

VALUES &
ATTITUDES

SISU

The word *sisu* is rooted in the word *sisä*, meaning "internal". Sometime during the Second World War, as the world watched Finland fight for its independence, *sisu* began to mean having guts, never quitting in the face of adversity, and soldiering on with pluck and a good helping of courage when things get tough. Combining these two definitions suggests that *sisu* really refers to our internal reserves of strength, the ones that kick in when we realize that we must never, ever quit.

Ever since those white-clad, Winter War soldiers erected blue and white flags in a show of Finnish independence, *sisu* has acted as a uniting cultural ideal. During *kaamosaika* (polar nights), when the days are the shortest and the nights are the darkest, Finns know that *sisu* will carry them through until summer. When a governmental or

educational policy just isn't working, Finns will tap into their collective reserves of *sisu* in order to accomplish change. And, likewise, when an immigrant is struggling to learn the grammatical complexities of the Finnish language, *sisu* will surely help them to succeed.

Every year, hundreds of events take place to test this feature of the Finnish character. The sauna world championships, in which the winner manages to withstand the heat of the sauna longer than his or her competitors—temperatures can be as high as 110°C (230°F)—is a test of stamina and stoicism. "Swamp football," wherein players run, kick and pass a football in mud up to their thighs, is another example. Extreme sports aside (you should search for videos on YouTube to see for yourself), *sisu* is the source of Finnish strength.

PROUD TO BE FINNISH

Finns are fond of saying, "*On lottovoitto syntyä Suomessa*" ("To be born in Finland is like winning the lottery"). They are proud to be Finnish, and loyal to their fatherland (*isänmaa*). They are, however, not without a sense of humor about the land they love: take a look at the comic "Finnish Nightmares," Roman Schatz's book, *From Finland with Love*, or "Very Finnish Problems," a satirical look at Finland in book form and on social media. Finns love Finland, but they love having an affectionate laugh at its expense, too.

Finns like to travel, often to escape the bitter cold of the winter months, but, in most cases, they are happy to return home. Where else can you be in the city one minute, and in the middle of a pine forest the next? Where other than Finland can you ski onto to the frozen waters of Lake Saimaa or Lake Päijänne? And, at home in Finland, you can enjoy *muikku,* deep fried sweet-water vendace fish, and *kalja,* beer, in summertime on those very same shores. Where other than Finland can you hear the Finnish language spoken all around you? Although it can be nice to fly somewhere warm once in a while, to witness other cultures first hand, to enjoy foreign bodies of water, Finland is home, and home is sweet.

Still, Finns often like to hear that foreigners— tourists, immigrants, returnees—enjoy Finland as much as they do. While you're here, you'll likely be asked things like, "How do you like Finland?" and "Why did you come here?" and "Have you tried *salmiakki* (salt liquorice) and did you like it?" Because they are modest, there may be a note of disbelief in these questions—why *would* you come here to this little Nordic corner of the world? And how *could* you like *salmiakki*? Of course, almost any response you provide will likely inspire pride and delight. After all, your interest in their country only confirms what they already know: that Finland is a wonderful, beautiful *maa* (country, land) and that *salmiakki* is delicious.

Finns are proud of the *Kalevala* and its heroes. They are proud of their unique and difficult language, and that it is one of the sources for J. R. R. Tolkien's Elvish language. They are also proud of things that are internationally recognisable, such as film stars with Finnish heritage, or of large corporations such as Nokia. In other words, they enjoy it when the rest of the world provides some acknowledgement of their many strengths. After all, they have done pretty well for themselves in the last hundred years or so.

In recent years, Finns have rightfully taken much pride in the quality of their education; Finland has consistently ranked near the top of the Programme for International Student Assessment (PISA) study since 2006, indicating that there is something special about Finnish education. Although Finland's PISA scores have dropped a bit since 2012, their education is still noted for its excellence, and teachers and scholars from around the world still look to the Finnish National Curriculum for cues on how to improve teaching and education policy.

Finland is also a country of regulations. Finnish society functions pretty well as a result of its clear rules and expectations, but it can also present some challenges. After all, sticking fastidiously to rules can be annoying at best, and life-disrupting at worst. When you want something done, you may be told, "*Meillä on sellaiset säännöt*", "Those are the rules." This tendency to abide by the rules has its benefits, however; it could be the reason for the lack of corruption found in government and bureaucracy.

DEMOCRACY

Finland is a republic and a mixed economy, with a parliament, a prime minister (who is the head of government), and a president (who is the head of state and of the armed forces). Currently, Finnish society falls somewhere between a meritocracy and a welfare state, providing opportunities both for career advancement and robust access to social security. This is made possible through high voter engagement, strong collective bargaining rights, universal access to education, and an entrepreneurial spirit.

Finnish politics comprises several major political parties, the largest among them being Keskusta (the Center Party), Kookomus (the Coalition Party), Sosiaalidemokraatit (Social Democrats), and Perussuomalaiset (The Finn's Party).

For Finns, democracy means both freedom and responsibility. They are conscientious citizens, who take their democratic duties seriously. They believe that, in order to change things, they have to act. It is indicative of the degree of participation that 80 percent of the Finnish workforce belong to trade unions. Collective pay negotiations are conducted between the central trade union organization, SAK, and the main employers' organization. Individual unions will negotiate the details once the main framework for pay rises and conditions has been agreed to.

As part of democracy there is the ingrained concept of meritocracy. You advance in society through your achievements, not through birthright. The key to advancement is education, where there is equal access and opportunity. Finland is, more or less, a classless society. Since the yuppie days of the 1980s there has been an emerging nouveau riche section of society with an ostentatious lifestyle that is heavily frowned upon by most Finns. But people still like to know how much others earn, and the annual list of highest earners and taxpayers is eagerly read. Most Finnish lottery winners wish to remain anonymous.

The aristocracy that marked the years of Swedish rule is a thing of the distant past, though the manor houses still stand and the families continue. A small number of Swedish-speaking Finns regard themselves as superior to Finnish speakers and maintain some of the aristocratic customs. Finns are ardent followers of other people's royalty, and stories about the royal houses from Sweden to Monaco sell newspapers. The "new royalty" are television stars and sportsmen and women. These days you can also be famous for being famous, as in the rest of the world.

Finns are keen readers—book sales are high— and they are well-informed about world affairs and politics, being avid consumers of news and newspapers. There are fifty-six daily newspaper titles with high circulation figures—a very large number for such a small population. The democratic decision making process relies on people being well-informed. Democracy is practiced from early days, school pupils having student councils. Parents are involved

Situated in the heart of Helsinki, Oodi pubic library is a modern testament to the Finns' deep love of literature.

in educational decision making. Student politics are still active, though there is growing concern about increasing apathy and a gradual decline in voter turnout. On the other hand, single-issue movements are growing in strength. Young Finns, for example, are particularly active in environmental issues.

EQUALITY

The Finnish constitution guarantees equality to all citizens, including equal rights for men and women. Finland, like the other Nordic countries, is often cited as being among the most gender-equal countries in the world. The number of women in public life is comparatively high, with Tarja Halonen perhaps being the most well known example internationally; she became the first woman president in 2000 after having served for many years as the Minister for Foreign Affairs.

However, the notion of total gender equality is still, in many ways, aspirational. Equal pay has not yet been achieved, and Finnish women still earn on average 20 percent less than men. In spite of these shortcomings, Finnish women embody the *sisu* ideal, and they are generally well educated and financially independent. Like in much of the rest of Europe, having a job and one's own money is an accepted norm for Finnish women. But even with high levels of education and opportunity, Finnish society has some way to go to achieve total gender equality.

The statistics on violence against women make for uncomfortable reading. This is also true of the very high unemployment rate among immigrant women, even when compared with their male counterparts. Rape within marriage was only criminalized as recently as 1994, though Finnish women have enjoyed greater equality outside the home for much, much longer. It seems that, with all the equality that Finnish women have by right, there are still some strongly pervasive elements in Finnish life that many in the West would identify as sexist.

HONESTY

For years, Finland has ranked extraordinarily low on political corruption; for example, they fell within the top three least corrupt nations in the world in 2018, according to Transparency International's corruption perceptions index. Aside from some unsightly blemishes on this record, Finnish government has a reputation for honesty.

The same is largely true of Finnish society as a whole. Honesty and forthrightness are important values, and this is likely to be evident in your interactions with Finns. It's also visible in the surprising degree of trust that Finns have in each other. For instance, you will notice that they are often unconcerned about leaving possessions, sometimes even valuable ones, unattended for a little while. One notable exception to this is bicycles; if you happen to be in possession of one while you're in Finland, lock it up tightly wherever you leave it.

Complete forthrightness does not extend to everyday business or social interaction, however. In many areas of the country, Finns are likely to be cautiously polite rather than bluntly outspoken, particularly with non-Finns. In other words, they might not be the best at giving you feedback on your job performance, or telling you what they really think of your new haircut.

COMMUNITY SPIRIT

Within many aspects of Finnish life, community spirit is strong. Although it results in high taxation, Finns support each other and their society through a relatively comprehensive welfare state. In practice, this means that healthcare, unemployment benefits, and education are all guaranteed to be either free or extremely affordable. This welfare state and all it provides Finnish citizens is thought to be something of a right, although austerity measures and a greater resistance to high taxation have begun to chip away at these provisions.

Even so, the Finnish community spirit still thrives in traditions such as *talkoot* (short for *talkootyö*, or "volunteer work") whereby neighbors and friends volunteer to help each other with construction projects, home renovations, and gardening. This tradition dates back to a time before Finnish modernity, when life was decidedly tougher. If you are ever to attend a *talkoot*, you're sure to be rewarded for your labor with beer and something to eat, in addition to good company and a warm feeling of accomplishment. This concept of community and of mutual responsibility is an important pillar of Finnish society, and you'll see that many community enterprises, such as festivals and events, are made possible through volunteer work.

PERSONAL RELATIONSHIPS

The Finns pride themselves on their introversion. Have a look at the Web comic "Finnish Nightmares" and you'll see how Finns tend to view everyday interaction, albeit at a comical extreme. Introverts the world over identify with "Matti," the Finn whose shyness makes it

WHEN YOU WANT TO LEAVE YOUR APARTMENT BUT YOUR NEIGHBOR IS IN THE HALLWAY

difficult to ride in elevators with strangers, engage in frivolous small talk, and the like. As reported in the *New York Times*, Chinese introverts have adopted Matti as something of a mascot, and coined a Mandarin word, "*jingfen,*" or "spiritually Finnish." Although Matti is the stuff of stereotypes, he's also a symbol of the way Finns see themselves.

Finns are equally proud of their loyalty in friendship, a reward for finally reaching intimacy with them. Of course, if you want to truly become a Finn's *ystävä*, friend, it's a good idea to learn some Finnish. Although most Finns speak impeccable English, learning a few words can go a long way. And forget what you've heard (or even what Finns will tell you!): Finnish is difficult, but not impossible, to learn.

The divorce rate in Finland is relatively high, but this does not represent a dearth of love or relationships. People tend to meet each other through clubs and associations, exercise and language classes and, of course, the Internet. If you find yourself isolated, give one of these options a try. If you're shy or introverted, remember Matti from "Finnish Nightmares, " and you will feel right at home in Finnish social life.

THE CHURCH AND RELIGION

Although it's a very secular nation, Finland has two national religions: the Evangelical Lutheran Church of Finland, and the Finnish Orthodox Church. Approximately 70 percent of the Finnish population belong to the Lutheran Church, which has seen an approximate decline of 10 percent in membership over the past decade. Only 1 percent of Finns are members of the Orthodox Church. Members of both institutions must pay an income-based church tax of between 1 and 2 percent, depending on the municipality—the tax is often cited as a major reason for leaving. Another reason is the Church's ambivalent stance on LBGTQ+ rights. While some members of the Church leadership belong to the LBGTQ+ community, the Church has been hesitant to state explicit support, something the Lutheran Churches of neighboring Sweden, Norway and Denmark have done.

Inside Turku Cathedral, the seat of the Lutheran Archbishop of Finland.

Despite the decline, the Lutheran Church remains an important institution in Finnish life. It provides community services such as free marriage counseling (even for non-members), and still provides the backdrop for baptism, marriage, and funeral services for a significant majority of Finns. Although there are fewer and fewer parishioners filling the pews on Sundays, there are still plenty of Finns who turn to the Church to mark their lives' major milestones.

ATTITUDES TOWARD FOREIGNERS

You will find that many Finnish people are open, friendly, and interested in who you are and where you come from. As a very homogenous culture for which immigration is still quite new, however, tourists and immigrants alike may occasionally run into the odd uncomfortable situation. For example, people may stare at you because you look different, but this is usually out of curiosity, rarely hostility. Like most places, however, racism exists, and there have been isolated incidents of racially motivated violence. The majority of Finns condemn racism and xenophobia.

Long-term residents and refugees are provided with an immigration plan upon moving permanently to Finland to aid their integration. This usually includes intensive Finnish language classes as well as career training. Short-term residents usually don't require a comprehensive integration plan and are not provided with these services.

CHAPTER THREE

FESTIVALS, CUSTOMS, & TRADITIONS

NATIONAL CELEBRATIONS

If you see the Finnish flag flying in front of public buildings, you'll know it's a special day. All Finnish holidays are *liputuspäivät,* flag days; however, there are additional flag days that are not public holidays, such as Mother's Day, on the second Sunday of May. The majority of national holidays are of Christian origin. Others, however, like Vappu, marking the end of winter, or Midsummer's Day, tie the Finnish calendar to the cycle of the seasons.

Epiphany (Loppiainen)

Epiphany (January 6), is a public holiday. It marks the official end of Christmas. There are no particular festivities related to this day, except in church. Most people take down their Christmas trees on this day.

Good Friday (Pitkäperjantai) and Easter (Pääsiäinen)

Good Friday and Easter follow the Western Church calendar, although some of the customs related to celebrating Easter have come from the Orthodox tradition. On Palm Sunday (Easter Sunday in western Finland), children go door-to-door dressed as witches, wishing their elders good health, and receive chocolate in return for a decorated willow branch. The tradition dates back to a time when mischievous spirits and witches were thought to wonder the streets before Easter, looking for trouble.

Mämmi, the traditional Finnish Easter dessert, is eaten alongside *pasha*, the traditional sweet pudding marking the end of Lent in the Orthodox tradition. Finns decorate their houses for Easter, and it is traditional to grow some grass in a dish to symbolize the new growing season. Ascension Day and Whitsun (Pentecost) are also public holidays, the dates varying in accordance with Easter

Runeberg's Day (Runebergin Päivä)

On February 5 the Finns mark the birthday of the national poet, Johan Ludvig Runeberg, and eat traditional cakes named after him. Known as *runebergintorttuja*, these are small, cylindrical cakes topped with raspberry marmalade and powdered sugar.

Kalevala Day (Kalevalan Päivä)

Kalevala Day, also known as Finnish Culture Day, is on February 28, marking the day when the compiler of the oral tradition, Elias Lönnrot, signed and dated the initial version of the national epic. A number of events to celebrate the *Kalevala* and the Finnish language take place all over the country.

International Women's Day (Kansainvällinen Naistenpäivä)

On March 8, Finns celebrate women and women's rights by giving flowers and presents to the women in their lives.

April Fool's Day (Aprillipäivä)
April Fool's Day is marked by news stories that test people's credulity.

May Day (Vappu)
May Day (May 1) is a public holiday. It is a celebration of many things: the end of a long winter, workers' rights and socialist traditions, as well as student life and higher education. The celebrations start on the eve of May Day, or Vappuaatto. This typically involves eating warm weather fare, such as sausages (*nakit*) and potato salad (*perunasalaatti*), desserts such as sugary doughnuts (*munkit*) and funnel cake (*tippaleipä*), in addition to drinking lots of beer and sparkling wine.

Graduates don their white caps at the jovial May Day celebrations.

This is a lively, community-centered drinking festival with elements of carnival—balloons, funny hats, and a lot of noise. Traditionally, May Day marks the official beginning of spring, originally celebrated on May 14, Flora's Day. Local choirs usher in the spring through song in the morning, while political and trade union activists organize town marches and political rallies. It is customary for graduates of higher education to wear their white, Nordic-style student caps. Lunching in a restaurant is another May Day custom, and menus often include a lot of salted fish, to cure the hangovers from the night before!

Midsummer's Day (Juhannus)

Midsummer's Day falls on the nearest Saturday to June 21, the longest day of the year. Midsummer marks the annual *yötönyö* (nightless night), when the sun doesn't set at all in the north of Finland, and the sky remains a dusky blue and pink even in the far south. The magic associated with midsummer has roots in pagan fertility rites, but it is also in part a celebration of warmth and light after a long, dark winter. Midsummer, in contrast to May Day, is usually celebrated in the countryside. On the eve of Midsummer (*juhannusaatto*), there is usually a mass exodus from towns and cities for lakeside summer homes, nestled in the forest. Even Helsinki can be very quiet, though traditional celebrations with bonfires and outdoor dancing are organized

Basking in the summer warmth, onlookers enjoy the pleasing spectacle of a Midsummer bonfire.

in the Seurasaari outdoor museum area. As in all Finnish secular celebrations, a great deal of alcohol is consumed, usually in the heat of the sauna, or by the shores of a lake.

All Saints' Day (Pyhäinpäivä)

All Saints' Day takes place during the first weekend in November. On this day, Finns acknowledge the dead by placing candles on the graves of family, friends, and ancestors. A sea of candles can make for a beautiful sight on dark November night.

Independence Day (Itsenäisyyspäivä)

December 6, marks Finnish independence from the Russian Empire in 1917 after more than 100 years

Finnish students particicpate in a cavalcade to mark Independence Day.

of occupation. The day usually takes on a somber, patriotic tone, and Finns express gratitude for the country they live in

A televised reception is held each year at the Presidential Palace, where Finnish celebrities of all stripes are dressed to the nines. The press reports on all aspects of the celebration, but particularly the fashion on display (this event is something like the Finnish version of the Oscars).

Christmas (Joulu)

The most important day of the Christmas season is Christmas Eve, or Jouluaatto, on December 24. This is when Finns eat Christmas dinner, which usually consists of roast ham, carrot, potato, or rutabaga casserole, ginger cakes and biscuits, and, of course, mulled wine (*glögi*). After an early Christmas meal, Finnish children receive gifts—directly from Santa Claus himself! The Finnish Santa does not bother with chimneys, preferring to walk straight through the front door. This is because almost every family has their own Santa; typically, a family member or friend dresses up and delivers presents to the children of the house.

Christmas Day and Boxing Day (Tapaninpäivä) are usually uneventful, public holidays. Most shops, restaurants, and public offices are closed on Christmas Day, but things are changing: you'll find that more and more public places remain open every year.

New Year's Eve (Uudenvuodenaatto)

December 31, New Year's Eve, is a big celebration in Finland, complete with fireworks displays, eating and drinking with friends and loved ones, and partying, either at home or out on the town. Usually, the night either begins or ends with a sauna turn. One old custom still practiced by many on New Year's Eve is melting tin horseshoes. The melted tin is cast into a bucket of snow or water, and then the shape is interpreted in the shadow of a candle to predict what the new year will bring.

New Year's Day

New Year's Day is a public holiday. The president makes an annual address to the nation, which is broadcast on radio and on television.

Love your wife? Celebrate your romance by throwing her over your shoulder and dragging her round an obstacle course for an hour.

FESTIVALS

As you have probably guessed by now, summer is a cherished time in Finland. It is short, full of light, and glorious (when the weather is good). Because it's a special time of year, there are hundreds of outdoor festivals and events that take place all over the country. There are music, theater, folklore, poetry, dance, and visual arts festivals, along with hundreds of sporting events, from rowing to wife-carrying! Most municipalities organize one or more music festivals a year, some of which are widely

Musicians perform at the Kaustinen Folk Music Festival.

known and draw audiences from around the world.
They range from opera in Savonlinna to jazz in Pori,
from folk music in Kaustinen to tango in Seinäjoki, and
from rock in Joensuu to chamber music in Kuhmo.

The Opera Festival hosted in Savonlinna, an
idyllic lakeside town, is internationally recognized
and attracts many important names in the genre.
Finnish singers and visiting opera stars perform
in the medieval castle of Olavinlinna, located on
an island in the middle of town. Each year sees the
premieres of new operas, attended by connoisseurs
and laypeople alike. In Savonlinna you can enjoy
the specialty of fried vendace (*muikku*), a local
fish, on Muikku Terrace overlooking the lake on
Midsummer's Eve, or a five-course dinner at the

Oopperakellari, alongside the singers you have just heard at the opera.

Pori Jazz Festival has attracted some of the leading jazz musicians of the world, including such artists as the late Miles Davis, Herbie Hancock, and The Manhattan Transfer. The festival doesn't stop at jazz, though; there have been plenty of performers outside the genre, like Bob Dylan, Stevie Wonder, Alicia Keys, and B.B. King. There's something for almost everyone at Pori Jazz, which probably explains why it is one of the oldest and best attended festivals in Finland.

Ulkomaalainen (foreign) cultural commentators have often noted the incongruity of the stoic, sometimes even somber, nature of Finnish culture and its love for tango. Finns, however, have made some modifications to the Argentinian dance, thereby making it their own. For one thing, Finnish tango is written almost exclusively in a minor key, giving it a certain melancholy sort of *sisu*. Whatever the reason, Finns love to dance the tango, so the Tango Markkinat (Tango Festival) in Seinäjoki is a popular event. The festival consists mainly of dance competitions, but it is also a general celebration of this quirky aspect of Finnish culture.

Ilosaarirock, held in the North Karelian city of Joensuu, combines all varieties of rock into one spectacular outdoor music festival. Ilosaari has welcomed headliners such as Imagine Dragons, Portishead, Aphex Twin, Muse, and, of course,

Finnish symphonic metal favorite, Nightwish. The festival usually takes place during the second weekend of July, when Finnish summer weather is most likely to be at its best. If you are a fan of rock music and you enjoy multiday, outdoor festivals, this is the place for you.

Kuhmo Chamber Music Festival, started by the Finnish cellist Seppo Kimanen and his Japanese wife Yoshiko Arai, is one of the world's leading chamber music festivals. It is run by volunteers in the small town of Kuhmo, in the northeast of the country. There is a different theme each year, and over two hundred concerts take place over nine days and nights, with the venues ranging from old schools to the church. The festival made world headlines in the mid-1980s, when the talented Soviet pianist Viktoria Mullova defected to the West while performing at Kuhmo.

FAMILY CELEBRATIONS AND RITES OF PASSAGE

Rites of passage marked by established customs vary by family and region. Even so, there are a number of traditions that are universal.

Despite growing secularism, for what is still a majority of Finns, a christening or baptism will take place when a baby is around two months old, and is traditionally when the child's name will be revealed by the parents. It is traditional to give a child at least two first names, the second often being one that runs in the family. Most names are associated with a particular day of the year, according to a special "name day" calendar. Most people choose names from this calendar, thus giving the child a name day to celebrate.

Celebrating name days is universal in Finland. The day is marked with presents from close friends and family, and lots of congratulatory cards, text messages and Facebook posts from others. In the workplace, it is customary, even expected, to mark your own name day by bringing in cakes or sweets to share with your colleagues.

Similarly, most people also celebrate their birthdays. Finns sing "Happy Birthday" ("*Paljon onnea vaan!*") to the "*päivän sankka*ri," "hero of the day," and serve fare that will surely satisfy a sweet tooth. Important age milestones in Finnish culture typically include turning eighteen and fifty. Eighteen years old is the legal drinking age in Finland, so turning this age involves a warm welcome into Finnish drinking culture through activities such as pub crawls and clubbing. In contrast, fiftieth birthdays are a celebration of longevity and of what's yet to come. Depending on an individual's wishes, fiftieth birthday parties can be large, extravagant affairs, where dinner is served with wine, followed by cognac or liqueur and, of course, birthday cake.

The majority of Finns are members of the Lutheran Church through their christening and confirmation. The latter usually takes place at the age of fourteen, and is achieved through confirmation school or camp, followed by Holy Communion. Families organize a party, and the godparents are expected to attend. Even though Finnish society is increasingly secular, most couples get married in church. Big weddings are fashionable. The wedding is preceded by hen (women-only) and stag (men-only) parties for the bride and groom respectively—usually riotous events involving dressing up and crazy activities planned by their closest friends to celebrate the end of their single lives. As in most other Western cultures, alcohol plays a starring role in these events.

Mother's Day, the second Sunday in May, and Father's Day, the second Sunday in November, are significant opportunities to celebrate parents and the role they have played in their children's lives. Valentine's Day, February 14, is not a romantic holiday as such; it's referred to in Finland as Friendship Day ("Ystävän Päivä"), and is the perfect chance to show any important person in your life how much you care.

In their second year of upper secondary school, as the top class leaves for the examination season, young people dress up in formal evening gowns to do some formal, partnered dancing. This day is called Vanhojenpäivä, the Day of the Elders. The outgoing students, those in their third year, go around town on the last school day on floats, throwing candy into the street and dressed up as clowns, political figures, memorable film characters, and the like, with banners bearing sardonic comments about their school and education. The idea is that everybody in town knows that they have finished school. This event is called Penkinpainajaiset, which, roughly translated, means, "sitting down on the school bench for the last time." Nowadays, however, that name has been shortened to "Penkkarit."

Graduation from upper secondary is celebrated by a ceremony at school, followed by a party with the family, after which graduates and their friends usually move on to a local restaurant or bar. This is a poignant day for them, heralding as it does the loss of daily contact with their school friends. However, they can take comfort in the dozens of white roses given to them by party guests and in the promise that awaits them.

The Day of the Elders celebration ball—not your average student party.

CHAPTER FOUR

MAKING FRIENDS

Finns are notoriously difficult to get to know; they aren't big on small talk, especially not in English. It is said, however, that once you make a Finnish friend, they'll be your friend for life. You might be taken aback by how long budding Finnish friendships remain acquaintanceships, but putting the work in will reveal a staunchly loyal person on whom you can rely through thick and thin.

Gaining acceptance into a Finnish group of friends or colleagues can be tricky. Finns speak English exceptionally well, but it's not always their preferred language of communication. Learning the language, at least the basics, helps with this tremendously, however; Finns like to see that you've put the effort into familiarizing yourself with their culture, and that is often the first step in a developing friendship.

Then again, if you're really having trouble breaking through to a Finn whose friendship you'd like to have, buy them a drink. Or two, or perhaps

three. Alcohol can act as the great equalizer in
Finland, dissolving the social reticence that might
otherwise be present.

HOSPITALITY

Finnish hospitality begins and ends with coffee. If a
Finn invites you over to their place, you will arrive
there to find coffee already brewed or, at the very
least, ready to be brewed. Depending on age and
demographic, there's also a good chance that you
will be offered *pulla* (sweet buns) or cake to go with
it. Then, a chat around the coffee table will ensue;
this is what Finnish hospitality looks like.

Finns may also want to provide you with some quintessentially Finnish experiences, such as a stay at the *mökki* (summer cottage), perhaps for *juhannus* (midsummer). If you accept such an invitation, you will find yourself by a lake, under the shade of tall trees. You may catch the scent of *makkara* (sausage) on the grill, or the smell of wood smoke as the sauna warms.

You'll notice the alluring way that the sun sparkles on the water of a Finnish lake, and the giddy summer atmosphere that seems to enchant your hosts. The sauna's dry heat will relax you, and a dip in the lake will restore you. After working up an appetite, you'll eat that *makkara* with some salad and potatoes, followed by *pulla* and coffee. You'll likely have already been drinking beer and *koskenkorva* (a very Finnish brand of vodka), and so that summer giddiness will have infected you, too. Missing modern amenities like electricity and running water will seem like unnecessary luxuries, as the sun remains in the sky or on the horizon all night. This, too, is what Finnish hospitality looks like.

Perhaps the Finns you encounter will want to take you out to eat at their favorite restaurant. If they invite you, they will almost certainly pick up the tab; if you invite them out for a meal, be prepared to foot the bill. If this meeting is mutually agreed upon, and it's unclear who invited whom, the bill should be divided equally. This rule holds regardless of gender. This is what Finnish equality looks like.

As an addendum to this section, it should be noted that only very close friends and family come calling on each other without having first agreed to a meeting, or at least having called in advance. So, if you have reason to visit a Finn at their home, be sure to let them know beforehand.

CONVERSATION AND CULTURE

Contrary to the stereotype, many Finns love talking.
When you sit in a café in a marketplace there will
be lively conversation and laughter all around you,
particularly in the summer. In the winter it is hardly
surprising that most people want to hurry back
indoors and don't stop to chat for long.

The stories about Finns who don't speak much,
or who get annoyed if you talk too much, are mainly
myths. Maybe it is simply that foreigners don't like

silence. The pace of conversation may be slower than you are used to, and there will be periods of silence—with which the Finns are comfortable.

Although the general Finnish mood may be melancholic, among friends Finns love to laugh, joke, and exchange funny stories. There also can be strong regional differences; for example, the eastern Finns of Savo and Karelia are more talkative than the people of western Finland. Wherever they may be from, Finns love to talk about their lives, the people in it, and the world around them. The best place to do this is at the lakeside, with your toes in the water at the edge of the jetty after a sauna on a summer's night, with long periods of silence—but the silence signifies awe and appreciation of the beauty around you, not that there is nothing to say. The silence won't last too terribly long, however, as the consumption of alcohol releases Finnish tongues.

Many Finns love to talk about sports. So, if you want to be popular, take an interest in ice hockey, or Finnish footballers abroad, or the continuing success of Finns in motor sports—just don't mention any embarrassing losses to Sweden.

Stand-up comedy is gaining in popularity. For example, Ismo Leikola, a Finnish stand-up, took the comedy world by storm in 2014 after winning the title of "Funniest Person in the World" at the Laugh Factory in Hollywood, California. Leikola's humor relies on interesting, everyday observations, typically about language oddities and idiosyncrasies, such as idioms or commonly used vocabulary. (Check out his video on the Finnish word "*niin*" and you'll see what I mean).

However, most Finns don't want to stand out in a crowd. This shyness is often the reason for the silence in public places. People talking loudly in public are frowned upon or thought to be drunk. That said, you may notice that Finns talk loudly on their cell phones.

FORMALITY VERSUS INFORMALITY

Finns are usually fairly informal in their dress and in their customs. It has been said that the new Finnish national costume is the tracksuit. Formal dress or Sunday best are usually fairly understated. There are occasions when the Finn will don a suit, but very few. Finns think nothing of appearing naked with the same sex, whether it is in the sauna (more on this topic later) or in the changing room of a public swimming pool. Perhaps this is one reason that Finns don't feel particularly compelled to dress formally for work or events: they've already seen each other naked!

Finns are on first-name terms with all their family and colleagues. Titles used to be important, but are far less so now. In fact many people do not use their titles except on their curriculum vitae or in a professional context.

The words *herra* (Mr.) and *rouva* (Mrs.) are almost never used, and children call their teachers by their first names. There is a movement toward teaching young people more formal behavior, particularly if they need to deal with their counterparts in central Europe, where the rules are different. Still, Finns feel most comfortable using first names and, if you spend some time here, you will too.

ALCOHOL AND ENTERTAINMENT

Alcohol is an integral part of Finnish social life, and Finns enjoy partaking. If you are having coffee in a Finnish home, you may be offered a glass of brandy, cognac, or liquor. At the lunch table, many Finns drink milk or *piimä* (buttermilk, or fermented milk) rather than something alcoholic. At business lunches, colleagues do not usually drink alcohol, although they may drink a great deal together at social events and work celebrations. Finns do not drink if they have to drive, and this is an acceptable excuse to abstain from alcohol, as is pregnancy, or being on medication.

During and after a sauna, Finns will usually offer you a glass of beer or a shot of something stronger. Finns drink *kuohuviini* (sparkling wine) at celebrations such as birthdays and weddings, but beer and vodka are usually also available.

As you might imagine, frequent alcohol consumption can present a public health problem. That said, the World Health Organization doesn't seem terribly worried about Finland; for example, Finland ranked 18th in the world for per capita alcohol consumption, putting them far behind Moldova, Lithuania, and Russia. Finns like to drink, but perhaps not as much as the stereotype would have you believe.

GIFT GIVING

Finns have been brought up never to visit someone empty-handed. A typical gift is a bouquet of flowers, although this is more common amongst older generations than young people. However, the demand for flowers is still significant, and there are plenty of florists in Finland who can create a beautiful, personalized bouquet on demand and in minutes. Other common gifts you might bring to someone's house include chocolates (usually Fazer *sininen*, Finland's favorite chocolate bar!), sweet buns (homemade or store-bought), cookies, or a bottle of alcohol. In other words, your gift will be well received if it is beautiful, sweet, alcoholic, or perhaps all three at once. It's also true that Finns appreciate gifts from other lands, so if you come bearing food or an artifact from your own culture, your hosts will surely be pleased.

JOINING CLUBS AND SOCIETIES

Foreigners can join any clubs or organizations
they wish, including political parties. If you find
yourself feeling isolated or alone in Finland, joining
a club, sports team, gym, language class, or activist
organization can be a great way to meet people.
Because Finns aren't the most open and gregarious
people, finding friends can require effort on

your part. Fear not, though: a lot of Finns join
organizations like these for just that reason, too. If
you join a group like the ones mentioned, you're
sure to find some like-minded folk.

CHAPTER FIVE

THE FINNS
AT HOME

QUALITY OF LIFE

Finns enjoy a very high quality of life. Finland
routinely ranks highly according to OECD quality-
of-life criteria, and it's not hard to understand why.
The environment is clean, and the singular beauty
of Finnish nature offers plenty of opportunities for
recreation and exercise. Finnish welfare and social
support is fairly robust, which allows people a safety
net upon which they can rely while pursuing their
dreams. Furthermore, Finland is a safe place to be;
it is low on crime, so people can go about their lives
without fear or anxiety for their physical safety.

A demonstrative example of the high quality of
life in Finland is the government-provided maternity
package, or as it is perhaps better known, the Finnish
Baby Box. This box of about fifty items has been
provided to all expectant mothers in Finland since
the year 1938. It contains clothes, reusable diapers,

toys, and almost anything else a new mother might require in caring for her child. In fact, the box in which these item are stored doubles as a bed for newborn infants. Every year, different styles and aesthetics are chosen for the items inside,

inspiring a lot of anticipation on the part of a mother-to-be. But, one thing remains the same: the package's contents are always gender neutral in color.

The maternity package is a symbol of the Finnish welfare state at its finest: efficient, useful, beautiful, generous, and appreciated. It's also a modest way in which to ensure that every single Finnish person starts out with the same baseline of material advantage. In other words, it's a rare Finnish child that starts life with nothing.

LIVING CONDITIONS

The Finnish quality of life is further enhanced by the excellence of Finnish design. Finns are very particular about their houses and their interiors, often spending a lot of money and effort on crafting a comfortable, beautiful home. Public buildings echo the appreciation of quality and beauty that is so apparent in Finnish homes. Finnish design is world famous, with household names including the architect Alvar Aalto, the Hackman design group, glass manufacturers Iittala, and the textile giant Marimekko.

The Finnish winter dictates the standard of the country's architecture. With winter temperatures dropping as low as -22°F (-30°C), houses have to be well built. The traditional wooden houses of the past have given way to ultramodern buildings, usually with a *"funkis"* (functionalism) inspired style. However,

beginning in the 1970s, reports of poor air quality in certain public buildings and private homes became more frequent. These problems are thought to be caused by mold, a result of excessive moisture. In the intervening years, many structures have undergone extensive remodeling, or have been torn down, in response. Even today, Finland struggles to strike a balance between protecting architecturally significant buildings and eradicating what they see as a major health problem.

In spite of this, Finnish homes are generally well built and well maintained. Living conditions are decidedly high. Whether in a family home or an apartment in the city center, Finns prefer to have a balcony or a terrace where one can sit and enjoy the warm air during the brief summer months. The overall cost of living is high, but Finns are generally highly educated and benefit from relatively high wages

Town planning is highly developed, incorporating land designated for leisure, special bicycle tracks or light traffic roads, and sports grounds. All Finnish towns are designed for the use of bicycles. Schools, hospitals, and health centers are modern and well equipped.

THE FINNISH FAMILY

The Finnish family is evolving. In fact, it's hard to describe what the "average" Finnish family looks like. The most statistically common family units, however, are opposite-gender couples, both married and cohabitating, with children and without. It's quite common for couples who live together but are not legally married to have children, while it's also common for married couples to have no children at all. In this respect, partners have a lot of freedom regarding what sort of family they choose to have. Additionally, as divorce in Finland is quite common, so too is remarriage and the creation of blended families.

Ironically, with the breaking up of so many nuclear families, genealogy is becoming a very popular hobby, helped by a combination of well-kept church records and the Internet. Over a million Finns have left Finland since the "hunger years" of the 1880s, many emigrating to the US and Canada. Their descendants, in turn, are seeking their Finnish roots. Cousins are sought and found all over the world, and families have big reunions.

Marriage between members of the same gender was legalized in Finland in 2017, as were adoption rights for same gender couples. Prior to this, registered domestic partnerships were legalized for same gender couples in 2002, but neither marriage nor adoption was yet permitted. This relatively recent legal milestone has made it possible for a new sort of Finnish family to emerge.

In the case of two-parent families, it's very likely that both parents work. New parents are guaranteed a long and generously compensated maternity or paternity leave, but, when the time comes to return to work, parents require support. As a result, municipalities organize and fund daycare centers for young children. Teachers who provide care to pre-school aged children are all trained and qualified in the field.

The birth rate in Finland is now at a record low of 1.4 children per woman and has been in steady decline the past seven years. Indeed, the country's population is now an aging one, since the annual number of births is below replacement rate. This is an issue of increasing concern for politicians.

DAILY LIFE AND ROUTINES

Finns are used to working hard: their ancestors eked a living out of a very hostile land. Work is highly valued, and it is through diligent study and work that a Finn gets ahead in society. In other words, the so-called Protestant work ethic is deeply ingrained. However, Finns with full-time positions generally work 35–40 hours a week, and holidays are generous by international standards.

There is an increasing gap between the "haves" and the "have-nots." Unemployment can be long-term and is particularly high in remote areas. The overall unemployment rate currently hovers around 7 percent. Additionally, social security benefits are not as robust as they once were, thereby increasing Finland's income inequality.

The Finnish working day generally starts between 8:00 and 9.30 a.m. in Finland. Many factories start at 6:00 a.m., but municipal and government offices open at 8 or 9:00 a.m., as do most schools. This also means that children are taken to day care early, before work. Most people have breakfast (coffee and porridge, yogurt, or bread with cheese, cucumber and tomatoes), read the news and check social media before going to work. Finns traditionally live close to their workplace, but increasing numbers of people now commute, especially from the Greater Helsinki area.

Lunch begins around 11:00 a.m. or 12:00 p.m., and the evening meal is usually served around 5:00

or 6:00 p.m., particularly in families with children.
Many people have their main meal at lunchtime,
and only a snack in the evenings. Unless otherwise
planned in advance, Finns generally don't visit other
people's homes late in the evening, so as not to
disturb them. Evenings after work are often a time
reserved for calm and relaxation.

FOOD

Finnish food commonly contains whole grains such
as rye and barley, as well as dairy, potatoes, fish,
beef, and pork. Sausages (*makkara*) are a popular
source of meat, whereas salmon is perhaps the most

commonly served fish, alongside Baltic herring, vendace, zander, and perch. Berries and mushrooms are also staples of the Finnish diet, and foraging for them is an established custom; this can serve both as an enjoyable hobby and as a way to stock up on delicious whole foods. These culinary elements are similar to other northern European cultures and reflect a climate that has traditionally been inhospitable to agriculture. However, technology and globalization have brought greater variety and choice.

While in Finland, you may find yourself munching on *karjalanpiirakka* (Karelian pastries), which, in spite of the name, are eaten all over Finland. These are small, savory pastries with a thin rye crust, filled with either rice or potato. They're delicious with cheese, tomato, or sometimes just with *munavoi* (egg butter, which is precisely what it sounds like, butter with bits of egg mixed in) spread over the top. Finns eat *karjalanpiirakka* for breakfast, as a light snack, or with coffee.

If you find yourself in the Savo region, you might just be served *kalakukko* (literally "fish rooster," or fish and pork baked inside a loaf of rye bread). *Kalakukko* may sound strange, but it's really a delicious culinary introduction to this region of Finland.

Fried *muikku* (vendace) are a summer specialty in much of Finland. These are small, freshwater fish that are caught locally and fried with a light

Fried *muikku* (vendace) with *karjalanpiirakka* (Karelian pastry).

rye crust. Then, they are eaten whole, usually with mashed potatoes. For Finns or long-time residents of Finland, this dish tastes of summer by the lake, or perhaps at the city harbor, enjoying the brief beauty that the season has to offer.

Whether you're in Lapland or elsewhere in Finland, you may encounter *poronkäristys*, or sautéed reindeer. This dish consists of thin strips of reindeer meat, sautéed with lard or butter, and served over mashed potatoes with lingonberry, fresh or preserved. As you might expect, reindeer is a gamey meat, one strong in flavor, which pairs well with buttery mashed potatoes and tart lingonberries.

If you are vegetarian or vegan, never fear; although most traditional Finnish foods contain meat and dairy, Finns are also health and environmentally conscious. If you live in or near a city, you should have no problem finding vegetarian options on restaurant menus, and vegan products, such as non-dairy cheeses, in supermarkets.

Finns also drink more coffee than any other nation in the world—over 24 pounds (11 kg) per person each year. They drink it in the morning, in the afternoon, in meetings, after the sauna, at weddings, and at funerals—it's a central part of daily life. When you visit a Finnish home, your host will put on the coffee right away. Finns are very particular about their coffee, preferring lightly roasted beans with a strong flavor. Most of the coffee in Finland is imported from Brazil, Colombia, and Costa Rica.

Remove Your Shoes

Finns take their shoes off when they enter a home, whether it is their own or someone else's. This is a custom that they take with them when they go abroad, and they are surprised to find that it is not a universal habit. A foreign visitor would not be expected to do so, but if you want to go native on this, the gesture would be appreciated. It is done for a practical reason—with the weather being what it is, the wet, mud, and dirt of the outdoors are confined to the hallway, keeping the rest of the house clean. Sometimes, at work or when going out, people carry with them a pair of indoor shoes to change into, leaving their winter boots beneath their coats. Again, this is a practical matter, as the boots needed to negotiate the slippery and icy streets are too hot to wear indoors.

The Sauna

The sauna is a sacred place for the Finns. Sauna is an almost religious cleansing ritual for the body and the soul. Whether in a home or at a summer cottage, the

sauna is among the most important rooms and often the first to be built.

Finland is home to over two million saunas, both traditional (wood-heated) and modern (electric). A traditional sauna is a small, wooden structure, often located near a lake or body of water. This kind of sauna contains a wood-burning stove, on top of which are hot stones; the fire heats the stones, and throwing water on them creates steam. After basking in the heat and steam for as long as you can stand, it becomes time for a jump into the lake or, in winter, the snow. Some of these traditional saunas have no chimney, leaving the smoke from the wood fire to fill

the sauna. These are known as *savusaunat*, or smoke saunas. A great many saunas, however, are electric, and are simply small rooms within a house or apartment. Whether wood-heated or electric, smoky or steamy, having a sauna is a restorative experience, and you should not leave Finland before giving it a try.

If you have never had a sauna before, get a Finn to show you what to do, and don't be afraid to try the famous birch twigs—they feel very pleasant and are good for circulation. Drinking too much alcohol in the sauna is not a good idea, but a beer or two is traditional. It is advisable not to eat before a sauna, but a good meal to follow it is a part of the ritual.

Remember to cool down well, and you will feel relaxed and cleansed.

A lot of social interaction takes place within the walls of the sauna. Meaningful discussions often take place between friends, siblings, partners, parents and children while in the sauna. Comfortable silences are perfectly common, too. Small talk (or avoidance of it) can be found within public saunas, among strangers. Business negotiations might happen within a spa, hotel, or rented sauna. Due to the nakedness inside the sauna, turns are segregated by gender, except among couples and, in some instances, family.

THE SUMMERHOUSE (*MÖKKI*)

The urbanization of Finland is a postwar phenomenon, and many Finns still yearn for rural life. They are prepared to drive long distances to escape the city in the summer, and are not put off by the traffic jams out of Helsinki on Friday, or Sunday on the way back. During the month of July, most Finns are on summer holiday, and life slows down for a spell. A lot of official business must wait for vacationers to return to work the following month, but Finns don't seem to mind; after all, everyone deserves a proper holiday.

Finns often retreat to a family summerhouse (*mökki*). There are 400,000 summerhouses, most of them located next to a lake, on an island, or by the sea. Each has its own sauna, of course.

Summerhouses are a very important feature of Finnish life and identity. Even people without access to their own cottage by the lake will likely have friends, relatives, or colleagues with whom they can tag along. The Protestant work ethic has its price, and burnout is a common consequence of stress. What better remedy than a Finnish summerhouse?

Typically, summerhouses are more primitive than the usual modern home. A trip to the summerhouse is an opportunity to get back to nature and live, voluntarily, without many modern conveniences, such as electricity and running water. Finns at the summerhouse bathe in the lake, use an outhouse, and rely on the nearly perpetual sun for light. Because modernity is, in the grand scheme of things, still relatively new, going back to the summerhouse and the nature that surrounds it is a little like going home.

SCHOOLS AND EDUCATION

The Finnish education system scores highly in international comparisons, coming top not only in exam results, but also in terms of cost per student. Over 90 percent of Finns graduate from post-primary education, and over 60 percent complete university degrees or their equivalent.

Compulsory education is free, and together with science and culture receives around 18 percent of Finland's budget. Local authorities are responsible for arranging general education, with regulations and partial funding from the central government. Preschool provision is available for six-year-olds, and compulsory education starts at the age of seven. The school year is divided into two terms, each having a week's holiday in the middle—a fall break (*syysloma*) in October, and a skiing holiday (*hiihtoloma*) in February or March.

Finnish children are independent from an early age. When the school year starts, in mid-August, it is common to see children learning their routes to school. After this they are not usually taken to school by their parents, but make their own way. In the sparsely populated countryside, as well as in districts where schools have been consolidated, municipalities provide free transportation to school if the journey is longer than five kilometers (just over three miles).

Education is held in high regard and is the source of social mobility. Finnish primary and secondary education consists of nine compulsory years and an optional tenth year. The school system is divided into the junior level (years 1 to 6) and senior level (years 7 to 9). Subsequently, students can apply either to upper secondary school or to vocational school. The aim of education in Finland is to provide a comprehensive overview in subjects such as Finnish, Swedish, or Sami (that is, instruction in the child's mother tongue), mathematics, history, geography, and foreign languages. Everybody has to learn Finnish, Swedish, and English.

Average reading skills are high, and young people's enthusiasm for reading as a pastime is strong. Well trained and highly professional teachers, the use of information technology, and a reading tradition are also contributing factors to the high literacy rate. Young people are avid users of technology and social media, thereby increasing their basic literacy skills, as well as, potentially, their foreign language proficiency. It is also thought that the subtitling of television programs strengthens reading skills.

School food is free for all in compulsory education. Young people are provided with a balanced, nutritious diet, and details of school menus are available to parents online.

Matriculation examinations happen nationally twice a year, in spring and in fall. Those who wish to go to university must score well in these exams, as well as on separate, program-specific university entrance exams. University admission is very competitive, and each year more young people apply to universities than there are places. Many continue in vocational schools or vocational universities, in which education is available for most trades and professions. In some cases, completing career training (in architecture, for example) qualifies students to apply for university.

At the age of eighteen the majority of Finnish men enter national service before going to university or joining the labor market. This usually means serving in the army for a short time, but it's also possible to complete this requirement through civilian service. Women can enter national service if they wish, but few do.

There are nearly twenty universities and art academies in Finland. Universities are state-owned and controlled by the Ministry of Education, but largely self-governing. The average length of university studies is four to five years, for which students are usually awarded a Master's degree. Financially speaking, students receive a great deal of support; the government pays a small monthly stipend in addition to providing state-guaranteed loans with extremely reasonable interest rates. The state also subsidizes student accommodation, health care, and meals.

Finnish universities boast a variety of international degree programs, to be completed entirely in English. For many years, these universities did not charge international students tuition at all. Since the year 2017, however, non-Finnish students who lack permanent residence or citizenship have been charged yearly tuition fees. However, universities offer very generous scholarships to a high percentage of students, so if you are interested in studying at a Finnish university, there's still a good chance that you will be able to do so free, or with some assistance.

Research and development is funded by both the state and the private sector. Particularly, technological and scientific research tends to be prioritized, as is currently the case in much of the world. Philosophy, Finno-Ugrian languages, social sciences, linguistics, forestry, and mathematics are also important areas of study. Open access to higher education is available through the "summer universities," institutions that organize university-level courses to the general public.

Finns are committed to continuing education, which is provided by local authorities, trade unions, volunteer organizations, and adult education centers in a variety of subjects. Lifelong learning and skill development also continues in the workplace. Retraining courses are available for the unemployed and to people who are in professions and trades that are changing or disappearing.

If you ask Finns what they consider to be the most important factor in getting ahead in life, most would say that it is education, reflected in the great number of resources they invest in it. Finland's success as a nation and as a culture is largely due to their successful education system.

MOVING TO OR VISITING FINLAND

If you are looking to rent an apartment or a house while you're in Finland, all the information you will need is easily accessible online. Tori.fi is usually a great place to start, and, if you'd prefer to work with a real estate agent, their information should also be readily available. Furnished apartments are available, but are, of course, more expensive.

If you're thinking of a shorter stay, there are hotels and hostels in nearly every city. Hotels tend to be on the expensive side, so hostels are a good option if you are on a tighter budget. The online rental Website Airbnb also offers numerous options at various price points.

CHAPTER SIX

TIME OUT

OUTDOOR ACTIVITIES AND NATURE

You have probably guessed by now that Finns love the outdoors. Regardless of the season, many Finns enjoy spending their free time in nature. In fact, each season comes with its own enjoyments and hobbies.

In the summer, spending time at a *mökki* (summer cottage) is a much loved pastime. Whether at the summerhouse or in town, summer activities may include swimming, hiking, boating and water skiing, biking, grilling and picnicking. Remember, in the land of a thousand lakes, you are not likely to be far from a body of water, and the same goes for forestland.

In the fall, many Finns like to forage for wild mushrooms and berries, and some enjoy hunting as well. Lapland is known for its stunning *ruska*, autumn foliage, and so many head north for hiking during these months. There is also an extensive

network of wilderness huts, which are free and open to all for overnight stays. The *ruska* of southern Finland is also quite lovely and itself worth exploring.

Winter brings with it a wealth of outdoor activities, particularly when temperatures are at their coldest. After the dark *kaamos* (polar night) months of November and December, when light slowly begins to return to Finland, lakes are frozen solid, and there is a thick blanket of snow covering the ground, it's officially the season for winter sports. Finns enjoy cross-country skiing, snowmobiling, snowshoeing, ice skating, and swimming (yes, swimming!). Some brave Finns enjoy taking a dip via a hole in the ice (*avanto*). This activity is usually preceded and followed by a sauna, of course.

Spring is a period of anticipation in Finland. As winter conditions slowly recede and excitement for the summer months begins to swell, it can be difficult to enjoy the outdoors. Springtime in Finland is notoriously rainy, and winter overstays its welcome almost every year. Even so, you may see people venturing out onto the ice for as long as it remains firm, and walking through the forest, even when the weather is poor. When much of the ice and snow has melted away and the sun returns, euphoria sets in and the Finns come out in droves, like flowers reaching toward the sun.

FREEDOM TO ROAM: EVERYMAN'S RIGHT (*JOKAMIEHENOIKEUS*)

Most Nordic countries place a high value on the concept of "freedom to roam," and have enshrined the sentiment in law. Freedom to Roam guarantees the right of all individuals to enjoy and make use of undeveloped countryside, even that which is privately owned. It is also a set of rules pertaining to the way in which this right is limited.

You may walk, ski, or cycle freely in the country, except in gardens and in the immediate vicinity of homes, and in fields or planted areas that could be damaged. You may stay or set up camp temporarily at a reasonable distance from homes. You may pick wild berries, mushrooms, and flowers as long as they are not a protected species. You may fish with a rod and line, but other kinds of fishing require a license. You may row, sail, use a motorboat, swim, or wash in inland waters and the sea. You may walk, ski, drive a motor vehicle, or fish on frozen lakes and rivers. You may not disturb the privacy of people's homes, for example by camping in unreasonably close proximity or making too much noise, nor disturb large game, breeding birds, their nests, or their young. Tourists in Lapland often wait in their cars while reindeer bask on the warm asphalt road (imagine the photo opportunities!).

You may not drop or leave litter, drive motor vehicles off-road without the permission of the

landowner, and you may not fish or hunt without the relevant permits.

Basically, enjoy your right to roam and forage for food, but make yourself scarce. Do not exploit nature for profit, or disturb the people or animals on your path.

SPORTS

Many Finns are sports mad, and generally, the madder the sport, the better. Facilities are good, and media coverage of all sports is extensive. There are sports for all seasons. Sailing, windsurfing, and waterskiing can be practiced all around the country. Winter sports are popular, Lapland being the best place for downhill skiing, though there are some very minor hills further south. Cross-country

Outdoor heated pools, such as the Allas Sea Pool in Helsinki, are open all year round.

skiing facilities are available everywhere, including Helsinki. You can skate in the open air and in ice stadiums. Golf has grown in popularity, and there are many excellent golf courses where a visitor may play as a guest. The most enthusiastic players have developed ice golf, which extends the short golfing season. Tennis is popular, played on both indoor and outdoor courts. Horse riding is a favorite, particularly with young girls. You can swim in lakes, rivers, and the sea, and there are, of course, well-equipped swimming pools in all the major towns and cities.

As for spectator sports, ice hockey is number one. In 1995, when Finland became world champions for the first time, the whole country came to a standstill. The victory was all the sweeter because it was against the Swedes, their arch rivals, in Stockholm, and the coach of the Finnish team was Swedish. The Swedes had been so sure they would win that they had pre-recorded their victory song "*Den glider in*" ("The puck slides in"). These words were printed on thousands of T-shirts in Finland. All these years later, this game still resonates in the annals of Finnish sports history. There are countless excellent Finnish-born hockey players, and many young Finns have become millionaires in the National Hockey League in the USA and Canada. Suffice it to say, in Finland, hockey is important.

Fans celebrate Finland's victory at the 2019 Ice Hockey World Championships.

Pesäpallo, or "Finnish baseball," is a popular summer sport. Invented in the 1920s, *pesäpallo* is based on American baseball, but it's hardly the same game. For example, the rules for pitching and running the bases are noticeably different, and there's quite a bit more running involved. With *pesäpallo*, Finns have made baseball their own, as they have with so many things.

Finns are also very fond of competitive driving, and rather good at it. The country has long produced fast rally drivers, although cynics would say that this is only natural for Finns who get plenty of practice on long icy country roads. With names such as Häkkinen, Salo, and Räikkönen in the world elite, Formula 1 competitions keep Finns glued to their television sets.

Cross country skiing has traditionally been a strong sport for the Finns, and everybody interested in winter sports knows about the ski jumpers. You need to be very brave, if not foolhardy, to participate in this daredevil sport.

Finland is a country of mass sports events; this is truly sport for all. The women's 10-kilometer run in Helsinki, many marathons, rowing, relay running from Lapland to the south coast, the Finlandia ski event, and many more attract huge numbers of participants. It is common practice to enter these events with a team of colleagues. Exercise is enjoyed by all.

DESIGN AND SHOPPING

Finland has excellent modern designers of furniture, dishware, and other products. Artek specializes in furniture by Alvar Aalto and glass by Aino Aalto, the power couple of Finnish design. In the first half of the 20th century, the Aaltos made an indelible impression

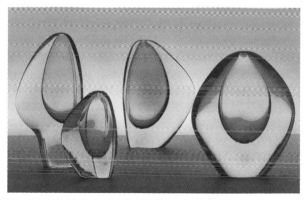

Examples of Finnish design: furniture by Alvar Aalto, kitchenware by Merimekko, and glass by Timo Sarpaneva.

on Finnish aesthetics, and their products can still
be found in homes all over Finland. In addition to
the Aaltos, look out for designs by Markku Kosonen
in wood, Anri Tenhunen in ceramics, Johanna
Gullichsen for linen products, and Ritva Puotila
for paper yarn carpets. Marimekko, known all over
the world for their unique textile designs, are also
a staple of the Finnish design aesthetic.

The main shopping streets in Helsinki are Pohjois-
Esplanadi and Etelä-Esplanadi for design products,
and Aleksanterinkatu for Stockmann and other large
department stores. Akateeminen and Suomalainen
Kirjakauppa are the biggest bookstores, and there
are also many antiquarian bookshops. You will find
art galleries and small shops in the pedestrian area
of Iso-Robertinkatu. Itäkeskus, Iso Omena, and the

A town's *tori*, market square, is a good place to find Finnish delicacies,
crafts, and souvenirs.

Tapiola center are also well worth visiting. You might like to check out the covered market, situated in the south harbor opposite the Palace Hotel. There you can find salmon—fresh, smoked, and cured—as well as the famous Finnish smoked hams.

In cities and towns outside of Helsinki, the main shops are typically in or near the center of the city, around the market square (*tori*). In the summer, the market square is abuzz with shopping and musical entertainment. Many towns have pedestrian-shopping areas where shoppers can browse unimpeded by traffic.

BANKS AND CASH MACHINES

Banking in Finland rarely takes place inside an actual bank, although there are times where that too is necessary. Making and accepting payments, checking balances, and checking account activity all takes place online, with the help of a username, password, and a book of key codes. This system has replaced many other payment types, including personal checks, which are no longer used. You may occasionally need cash, and there are plenty of cash machines around most populated areas.

However, banking can be a challenge for non-Finns. For example, getting Internet banking, which is used in a lot of instances of identity verification, sometimes requires an individual to have lived in Finland for a matter of months or years. If you think you'll be in Finland for a while and that you may need a Finnish bank account, research what is involved and what features you'll be allowed to access. The biggest banks in Finland are Dankse Bank, Nordea, and Osuuspankki. If you would like to open an account at one of these banks, you can make an appointment with someone who will help you to do so.

EATING OUT

Helsinki is famous for the quality and variety of its restaurants. The restaurant scene in other major Finnish cities can sometimes be lacking by international standards, but the Finnish palate is changing and developing. Wherever you are, you will surely find something delicious. Perhaps try the freshwater fish, or a gamey meat dish, if they are on offer.

Dining out in the evening is more expensive than eating out at lunchtime because almost all Finnish restaurants have a lunch menu aimed at working people on their lunch break. Lunchtime offers usually include a salad or a soup, a main course, bread, and coffee. Business travelers or tourists in search of a mid-day meal may wish to keep in mind that restaurants are emptier after 1:00 p.m., if they want to avoid the lunchtime rush.

Finnish menus usually indicate dishes suitable for vegetarians, as well as lactose- and gluten-free dishes. If you have an allergy, it is best to check the ingredients with the staff, but don't worry: food allergies are quite common in Finland, so they'll likely be prepared to accommodate your needs.

Helsinki has a long and vibrant tradition of café culture. The first café in Finland, Café Ekberg, opened in 1861 in Bulevardi and serves delicious cakes and pastries. Fazer Café on Kluuvikatu, owned by Fazer, the chocolate and sweets corporation, is also well regarded. For architectural ambience, you might try Ravintola Eliel at the railway station, designed by Finnish architect Eliel Saarinen.

There are few public restrooms. At cafés, you ask for the key at the counter, and there may be a charge. The letter M (for *mies*) on the door signifies the men's room, and the letter N (for *nainen*) is for women.

TIPPING
....

In general, tipping is not strictly necessary.
Rounding up the bill and leaving a little money
in appreciation of good service will always
be welcomed.

BUYING ALCOHOL AND DRINKING

For better or for worse, drinking alcohol is a
significant cultural practice in Finland. Alcohol can
be an effective lubricant in social interactions, as well
as a solo activity. The word "*kalsarikännit*" (literally
something like, "underwear drunkenness") has
gained international recognition in recent years,
putting Finnish drinking culture firmly on the map.
The notion of *kalsarikännit* refers to drinking at home,
in a state of undress, with no particular plans or places
to go: drinking at home, alone. Some might view this
notion as depressing or as an indication of alcoholism,
but not so the Finns (at least, not necessarily). It's just
that drinking can be done in a social setting or in
solitude, conspicuously or inconspicuously.

The state has a monopoly on the production and sale
of alcohol in Finland, and their outlet is the Alko stores.
Alko generally has a good selection of wines, beers,
and spirits, and their employees are knowledgeable and
willing to help with your selection. You can also buy

things like beer and cider from supermarkets and other stores. Alko stores are open Monday to Friday, 9:00 a.m. to 9:00 p.m. (smaller stores are only open until 6:00 p.m.); and Saturday, 9:00 a.m. to 6:00 p.m. Anyone over the age of eighteen can buy alcohol and get into most bars.

Beer, particularly Finnish lagers, are a very popular drink. Finns also enjoy vodka (their native brand, Koskenkorva, is quite popular), and gin has gained some notoriety with the release of the Finnish gin, Napue. "Long drinks" are a distinctive Finnish cocktail, usually made by mixing gin and grapefruit soda. There are also a lot of local producers of berry wines and liquors. One local delicacy particularly worth sampling is sparkling wine made from white currants.

Finns drink socially, but they also drink to get drunk. In fact, these two things are often one and the same; getting drunk *is* a social activity among friends and colleagues. There is wide social acceptance of drunken behavior. For example, loudness and raised voices when drunk is common in a society that otherwise values quiet. Finns of all ages drink to excess on occasion, and the summer festivals can be noisy and riotous. Finns are not prone to boasting, but they do brag about the severity of their hangovers.

Booze Cruises

"Booze cruises" from Finland to Estonia and Sweden are very popular. They have two purposes: drinking and fun. Many travelers don't disembark from their ship at all or for longer than it takes to buy some alcohol or to do a little shopping. When Finnish upper secondary students are preparing to leave school and to revise for their matriculation exams, they typically organize a student booze cruise. Teachers chaperone these trips, but usually that involves little more than drinking alongside their students. Even business meetings and negotiations take place on these cruises, as they're often an inexpensive alternative to a hotel. Colleagues and business associates drink the night away, and then wake up in the morning to conduct meetings.

Alcohol-related health and social problems are serious. While the state enjoys the revenue from the sale of alcohol, it has a responsibility for the nation's health and welfare, and sales are strictly controlled. However, recent legislation has loosened regulations related to the sale of alcohol, such as allowing supermarkets to sell drinks with an alcohol content as a high as 5.5% (up from 4.7%). This change has taken place while other Nordic countries are *tightening* alcohol regulations, putting Finland somewhat at odds with its neighbors in this regard.

NIGHTLIFE

Finnish youth learn to dance, and they learn to dance well. As young people, they learn to waltz, to tango, to foxtrot—and they grow up with these dances in their back pocket, to be pulled out when the time is right. Thus, a common way to spend the evening is to go to dance clubs. The music is often live, and the ladies' evenings, when women ask men to dance, are particularly popular.

If you aren't much for traditional dances and prefer more modern music, head for a nightclub. Helsinki and most major cities have a number of popular venues, and smaller cities usually have one or two.

In the run-up to Christmas, restaurants fill up with office parties (*pikkujoulut,* or "little Christmas") which are a chance to let your hair down with your colleagues. The office party season begins around the middle of November and extends well into December, when you'll notice that restaurants are often fully booked with several large parties on weekends. Of course, little Christmas largely revolves around the consumption of alcohol, alongside merriment and camaraderie, good food, holiday sweets, and dancing.

British- and Irish-style pubs are popular, and, in the summer, outdoor cafés and beer-drinking venues are all the rage. In cities with lakes, boat and pier bars on the water are wonderful additions to the summer nightlife.

SEX AND THE CITY

Finns are fairly liberated when it comes to sex, and women are nearly as likely as men to take the first step. With the growing number of single and divorced adults, casual sexual encounters are common. Dating and hook-ups can take place the old-fashioned way, at bars and clubs, or via dating apps like Tinder. In fact, the use of Tinder has increased dramatically over the last few years, eclipsing similar Finnish apps. Non-heteronormative dating can still be a challenge in Finland, as Finns are generally not quite as modern regarding sexuality and gender as they are in other matters.

CONFRONTATION

Finns tend to be averse to confrontation, and this extends to the realm of customer service. Therefore, they usually don't complain about bad service or a disappointing meal at restaurants, clubs, or bars. Just because they don't, however, doesn't mean you can't; most servers, cashiers and bartenders will be happy to assist you.

HIGH CULTURE

There is a great love of and interest in music of all kinds in Finland, and the country has a very strong tradition of musical education. Sibelius and the opera, particularly modern opera, are Finland's musical strong suits. Helsinki Opera House is one of the most modern in Europe, and there are numerous classical music festivals and events across the country all year round. Most towns have several choirs and at least one orchestra, a municipal art museum, and a variety of other museums. Helsinki and Tampere are the most famous theater cities, but all cities and large towns have a municipal theater, and usually many interesting art venues.

Some of Sibelius' contemporaries are being explored and are coming out of his shadow. Aulis Sallinen, Joonas Kokkonen, Kaija Saariaho, and Einojuhani Rautavaara are among the many who made their names in the latter half of the twentieth century, and there are a number of avant-garde composers. Experimental art and music are strong; once again, Finns can be found at the forefront of innovation.

A monument dedicated to preeminent Finnish composer Jean Sibelius by Eila Hiltunen at Sibelius Park in Töölö, Helsinki.

POPULAR CULTURE

Finnish popular culture is not well-known outside the country. Finnish art cinema is led by Aki Kaurismäki, who most recently picked up a Best Director award for his film *The Other Side of Hope* at the Berlin International Film Festival in 2017. Cinemas show films in their original language, with Finnish and Swedish subtitles. Most major American releases can be found in Finnish movie theaters, and Finnish TV stations are fond of airing Hollywood films.

Finnish popular music is quite varied. The Finns love tango and have developed their own tango culture. A Finnish tango is usually in the minor key, and the words tell of lost love and longing. Finns also love their own brand of rock, pop, and "*iskelmä,*" a style of pop music that is unmistakably Finnish. As you may already know (it might even be the reason you're reading this book), Finnish metal music is world-famous. Metal is a popular genre in Finland, and Finnish metal beckons tourists and immigrants alike. Give the bands Nightwish and Children of Bodom a listen, you too may have a headbanger inside waiting to get out.

As is the case in many other places, English-language music, often from the US or the UK, is also popular and receives wide exposure. That said, this doesn't seem to detract from the Finnish music scene, or to diminish the appreciation for culturally Finnish music.

Finnish metal band Nightwish hastening the apocalypse.

Finland has also produced at least one "Nordic Noir" gem of a television series, *Sorjonen* or, in English, *Bordertown*. The story follows protagonist Kari Sorjonen as he investigates murder and organized crime in the city of Lappeenranta, located on Lake Saimaa, close to the Russian border. (Incidentally, Lappeenranta is actually quite a safe city, endowed with a lot of natural beauty, and well worth a visit.)

CHAPTER SEVEN

TRAVEL, HEALTH, & SAFETY

Traveling within Finland is generally simple and headache-free. Public transportation like buses and trains usually run on time, although this is not always the case in bad winter weather. Traffic laws are strict, and Finns tend to follow them to the letter.

Finns keep to themselves when traveling and do not generally make small talk with the person sitting next to them. In fact, if they can help it, they prefer not to sit next to anyone at all. This leaves lots of time to gaze out the window and enjoy Finland's modern cityscapes and lush, green forests in quiet contemplation.

DRIVING

Finland is one of the mutually insured "green card" countries, and if you are driving yourself you will need an internationally recognized driver's

license. Traffic drives on the right, and passes on the left. Seat belts are compulsory for the driver and all passengers, and all motor vehicles must use headlights at all times, regardless of the time of day or weather conditions.

Most traffic signs are similar to those in continental Europe. Roads are kept in good condition all year-round—snow clearing, sanding, and gritting of roads are efficient, with fleets of snowplows out in the early hours during the winter. Only very rarely, when there is an exceptionally heavy snowfall or a sudden frost, do roads become impassable. You need to be cautious and drive at slowly if you are not used to winter driving. Special winter tires are obligatory from December to February, though they are permitted from the

beginning of November until after Easter and at other times when the weather conditions require their use.

The Finns are good drivers. They have produced several world champions in rally driving and in Formula 1, and they sometimes get carried away speeding on minor roads. There is a potential rally champion inside every Finnish driver. Speed restrictions are clearly marked, however, and fines for speeding are high. In fact, fines incurred for speeding are determined as a percentage of your income, and the more you make, the more you pay. Drivers going over the speed limit are usually caught by cameras on the expressway, and the legal implications and associated fines will be posted to you.

Try Your Luck

When someone asked Ari Vatanen—the many times world rally champion, and former member of the European Parliament—what makes a good rally driver, he answered, "A heavy foot and an empty head!" If you want to give it a go, there are a number of rally-driving centers around the country.

You can find gas stations all over the country, and you can obtain free maps showing their locations. When traveling in remote areas, however, ensure that you have enough gas to complete your journey. Most stations have automatic gas dispensers that take cash or credit cards and are open twenty-four hours a day.

Drinking and driving laws are very strict. Driving under the influence of alcohol or drugs is forbidden. The limit of alcohol allowed in the blood is 0.5 milligrams per milliliter, and infringement of this rule nearly always incurs a penalty in the form of a fine or imprisonment. When Finns go out to dinner or to a restaurant, they use taxis or public transportation to get home. Many people keep a personal breathalyser to check that they are safe to drive after a party. Police frequently use roadblocks, especially on Saturday or Sunday mornings, to check drivers for alcohol. Heavy drinking the night before can mean that you are still over the limit the following morning. Young Finns take turns being the designated driver on evenings out—"I'll drive this Saturday, and you drive next Saturday"—people don't take risks. Though expensive, taxi services are robust and available 24 hours in most areas.

One of the main hazards is the presence of animals such as elk and reindeer on the road, particularly at dusk and dawn. Watch out for warning road signs. A collision with one of these heavy animals can be very serious. In areas where the elk population is high, there are special fences to keep them off the road.

Be careful on summer evenings, as the low sun can seriously affect visibility. Most serious accidents are caused by careless driving. In case of an accident, call the general emergency number, 112, or local police on 10022. Police, ambulances, and rescue services are well organized and efficient.

TAXIS

Taxi stands are usually situated near major railway stations, shopping centers, airports, and, in smaller towns, by the main market square. Every taxi has a yellow sign (*taksi*) that, when lit, shows it's available for hire. Of course, all the information you'll need about ordering a taxi in your town can be found online. Cameras have been installed in most taxis to protect the driver.

CYCLING

Many Finns own a bicycle and use it all year-round. There are cycle routes, and in towns there are special marked areas of sidewalks intended for cyclists.

Children often cycle to school, and you see schoolyards with hundreds of bikes parked in special shelters. City bikes in Helsinki are free for use around town, on payment of a small deposit, and you can return them to any of the twenty-five bicycle ports in the town. Helmets are recommended, and you can rent one from the Helsinki city tourist office. Other towns run similar schemes—check locally for details. If you want to take your bicycle on a bus or a

train, you should check with the carrier; there may
be a fee.

There is a network of cycling routes around
Finland, marked by brown signs with a bicycle on
them, or you can find special cycling maps that
show the routes. Cycling is a good way to see the
country in the summer. Most of Finland, with its
gentle slopes, is ideal for cycling. In Lapland and
in eastern Finland there are some demanding hills,
and you need to be fit to manage them. The most
popular area for cycling tours is the Åland Islands,
where you can island-hop on ferries. Bicycle rental
is widely available. Check local tourist offices
for details. Remember a helmet, a cell phone, a
raincoat, and some spares, including a pump, before
you go on a longer trek. In-line skaters and roller
skiers also use cycle routes.

Cyclists and pedestrians should watch out for
snow falling from roofs in the spring. Slipping on
icy roads and sidewalks results in some 40,000
injuries a year, so be careful, and whether cycling or
walking wear shoes with good grip. In particularly
icy weather, studded shoes are advisable.

PUBLIC TRANSPORTATION

Public transportation is well organized in
Finland. Buses are the main form of local public
transportation in cities. Helsinki is the only city

in Finland with a metro network, and it also has trams. All public transportation timetables are available online. Popular apps to help you plan and purchase tickets for travel inside Finland include Moovit for navigation and transport options, VR Mobile for train tickets, and HSL Mobiililippu for all Greater Helsinki area travel.

Air Travel

Finland is well connected to the rest of the world by air. Most major airlines fly to Helsinki, and some international carriers fly to Tampere, Turku, and Rovaniemi. There are also many charter flights, particularly to Lapland.

The domestic airline network is one of the densest in Europe. Helsinki-Vantaa airport has excellent facilities, including duty-free shopping, Wi-Fi, and lots of charging stations for mobile devices. The main operator on internal routes is Finnair, and there are some other, smaller carriers.

Trains

Passenger trains serve most of the country except northern Lapland. Most towns are connected by rail, but traveling from east to west is more difficult than from north to south. All the main railway lines lead to Helsinki. Trains have special carriages for people traveling with pets, and storage for bikes, skis, and other large items. All intercity trains have restaurants on board, and many have conference

Helsinki's electric tram network is one of the oldest in the world and a great way to explore the city.

facilities. Sleeper services are available on all long-distance trains.

Coaches

Coach services cover more than 90 percent of public roads, and the timetables usually tie in with rail, air, and ship services. If you're unable to find a train that travels from one city to another, you can most likely find a coach that covers the route. You can buy tickets as you board, on the coach service's Website, or via ticket apps such as those provided by Omnibus.

Boats and Ferries

In addition to road travel, there are lake traffic routes in the summer, and boats to Sweden, Estonia, Poland, and Germany all year-round. Taking inland lake and river trips is a wonderful way to see the country. There is a coastal tourist route from Helsinki to Porvoo, and boats also go to some of the islands off the coast of Helsinki. The Åland Islands have a connecting network of shipping routes and ferries. You can also travel from Lappeenranta through the Saimaa Canal to Viipuri, in Russia.

WHERE TO STAY

Hotels are generally of a good standard, but this is almost always reflected in the price. Most have a sauna (it is Finland, after all) and many have a swimming pool as well. Hotels are plentiful, but the vast majority are run and owned by the same three chains: Sokos, Cumulus, and Scandic. If quality and comfort is your primary concern, Finnish hotels don't usually disappoint.

Other types of accommodation include spas, youth hostels, holiday villages, log cabins, and campsites.

There is also a wide choice of bed and breakfast accommodation and farmhouse vacations. You can also rent summerhouses and ski chalets. In Lapland, along the main hiking routes, you will find free wilderness huts you can sleep in.

HEALTH AND SECURITY

Finland has a good and efficient health service, with modern hospitals and health centers. The health-care system is a mixture of national and private care. Maternity care is among the best in the world, and the infant mortality rate is the lowest in the world. Dental care is good, but expensive as it is usually private. If you are staying in Finland for a while, it's a good idea to either ensure that your health care costs will be covered by Kela (the system handling all government benefits) or by your own private insurance. Although there are few serious health problems in Finland, the long dark winters can cause depression. Seasonal affective disorder (SAD) can be treated by special lights.

EU citizens have a right to health care under the EU agreements, and most Finnish doctors speak English. Most common remedies can be bought at supermarkets and pharmacies, where trained pharmacists also give advice on common ailments.

Finland is a very safe country. Crime rates are low. Bank robberies and burglaries are rare, though are unfortunately on the rise. Though pickpockets are few, it pays to be streetwise. You'll be pleasantly surprised by how safe and secure Finland is.

CLOTHING

The clothes you take to Finland will, of course, depend on the time of your visit. Windows are triple-glazed, and it is always warm indoors.

The winter is cold, and you will need a warm, windproof coat, hat, and gloves. Most important of all is footwear. Make sure you have shoes with a good grip, because slipping on the ice and snow causes tens of thousands of broken ankles and wrists in Finland every year. If you are going on a snow safari in Lapland, the tour operators will supply you with appropriate clothing. At ski centers you can rent all the equipment you need. Summers can be hot, but they can also be rainy and chilly, so be prepared for both possibilities.

As previously mentioned, Finns tend to dress casually, so there aren't too many reasons to pack especially formal clothing.

CHAPTER EIGHT

BUSINESS BRIEFING

GETTING DOWN TO BUSINESS

Finnish businesspeople are highly educated, very able, professional, and efficient. They usually know exactly what they are doing, and work hard to achieve their goals. They don't boast about it, but just quietly get on with the business at hand. The term "Protestant work ethic" could have been invented to describe the way they work.

Finns are also imaginative and innovative. They are good at foreign languages; indeed they have to be, as Finnish is hardly spoken outside Finland. They may appear to be serious or melancholy, but they're simply focused; don't take offense at this demeanor if you're in a meeting or working on a project with them.

One should keep in mind that Finland is still a relatively new society that has existed on the cutting edge of modernity for only a short time. Its rapid development from an agrarian economy to a highly advanced one has had far reaching implications for how Finns think and work. For the last few decades, Finnish society and education has placed a great deal of importance of the concept of *yrittäjyys,* or entrepreneurship. This has resulted in hugely successful endeavors such as Nokia and Kone, as well as significant innovations in the fields of science, engineering, and green technology. With Nokia's decrease in profitability and clout, however, Finland has been continually looking to regain some degree of its lost success story. If Finns have anything to do with it, they'll definitely succeed.

Likewise, it was not too long ago that Finland was largely isolated from tourists, immigration, and other global concerns. Now, the Finns are confronting not only their new position of success on the world stage, but also a society that is rapidly changing before their eyes. This presents challenges, but also stimulates their natural love of innovation and their relentless quest for improvement. This is why, when something isn't working, Finnish businesses will always be open to making changes and implementing solutions. Finns love novelty and hate inefficiency, and this has proven to be a winning combination.

OFFICE STYLE AND ETIQUETTE

Generally, the atmosphere in a Finnish office is relaxed and informal. Dress is casual, and suits are

worn for important meetings only. Finns are
serious about getting down to business. They feel
that working with others is not meant to be
entertaining—you stick to the business at hand.
They also assume that all the necessary information
is given, and that there is therefore usually no need
for any further questions or discussion. This last
assumption can result in confusion and a lack of
communication, but the flexibility of Finnish
hierarchy means that anyone in any position is
usually welcome to speak up and attempt to
clarify things.

People can be very frank with each other, but they can also be averse to confrontation. Here are some pointers in navigating this dynamic:

- Titles are usually not used. *Herra* (Mr.) and *rouva* (Mrs.) are used only if you don't know the person's first name.

- It is a good idea to learn to pronounce the names of your Finnish clients and business contacts correctly. This may sound difficult, but there are a couple of simple pronunciation rules that may help: always emphasize the first syllable, and one letter always corresponds to one sound. With a minimal amount of practice, you should be pronouncing Finnish names correctly in no time! As most foreigners regard Finnish names as difficult or even impossible, Finns are used to mispronunciations, but if you get them right they will be delighted.

- When meeting a Finn for the first time, they will expect you to shake hands with them. It is impolite not to do so. Then don't forget to shake hands again when you say good-bye. Once you know your business partner well, or if you meet frequently, it is not necessary to shake hands every time you meet, but do so if you haven't seen each other for a while. Additionally, Finns introduce themselves using their full name, first and last. They also answer the phone this way, but only when they don't know who is calling.

- Remember to introduce other people if they don't already know each other, regardless of age, gender, or position; introduce a man to a woman, a younger person to an older one, a person alone to a party of people, and a junior staff member to a senior one.

That's Just How It Turned Out!

Finnish comedian Ismo Leikola joked, upon returning to Finland after touring abroad, that Finns use the passive voice to describe things they themselves have done. So, if you try to praise your Finnish colleagues on a job well done, don't be surprised if they answer with something like, "Well then, that's just how it turned out!"

COMMUNICATION STYLES

Finns are considered introverts, and Finnish businesspeople are no exception, but with increasing globalization this stereotypically reserved style is changing. It has always been true, however, that Finns are honest and true to their word, and they expect the same of their friends and colleagues. This basic value has not changed, though the delivery may be different.

The Finns are naturally modest, often quiet, and, if asked for a comment, will usually pause to think before replying. They usually think in silence, and there is very little overt body language, so you should allow time for thought. Remember, Finns are comfortable with silence, even if you are not. Try not to fidget as it may come across that you are not paying attention. They may give a measured, slow response, which is a result of careful deliberation. In conversation, there is very little overlap in turn taking—in other words, it is considered bad manners to interrupt. While Finns on the whole may distrust those who seem to talk a lot, the Karelians and Savo people of the east are known to be more open and talkative. Being matter-of-fact with all Finns pays off well as they generally take things at face value.

The Finns are not always very diplomatic, because they state the truth of the matter without beating around the bush. Sometimes this may sound very blunt and categorical, but this is not intentional—it is just the Finnish way.

To sum up, the Finns are by nature reluctant communicators, but they have learned to function in a global business world. Part of this is making sure the general population is proficient in English; in fact, it is pretty much guaranteed that your Finnish business contacts will speak it very well. Knowing the global lingua franca helps a lot when your native language is barely spoken outside of your borders. However, this is precisely why you should learn some Finnish, if only a word or two. Finns always appreciate it immensely when their linguistic background is acknowledged.

Typical greetings include "*hei*" (hello), "*terve*" (health), and "*moi*" (hi—this one is fairly informal, so use it with caution). If you'd like to ask someone how they're doing, just say, "*Mitä kuuluu?*" (literally, "What is heard?"). When asked this, Finns usually respond (at least to those who don't speak Finnish very well—if you learn a bit more of the language, they may decide to be more honest!) with, "*hyvää*" (or, "good", that is, "good things are heard"). When departing, simply saying, "*hei hei*" is sufficient.

Finns who work in the business sector tend to have an awareness of and an appreciation for other cultures and communication styles. Therefore, you shouldn't need to worry about getting everything right—they will meet you somewhere in the middle.

Reluctant Communicators

A Finnish schoolteacher asked an English colleague whether he had any problems with children speaking in the classroom. The Englishman said, "Yes, I can't get them to shut up!" The Finn remarked that her problem was getting the children to speak.

PRESENTATIONS

Finnish presentations are usually well prepared in advance, with little deviation from the content of their notes or slides. They can also lack, shall we say, entertainment value; Finns are interested in the facts and not in holding your attention, necessarily—that's up to you. Like many of us, they can also appear to be visibly nervous, particularly if they are not confident in their spoken English skills. If you listen without appearing to be distracted, however, they'll greatly appreciate it.

If you are giving a presentation to a room full of Finns, remember to stick to the relevant information at hand, and try to present it in a straightforward way. Finns also mistrust what they perceive to be

bragging or gloating, which, in other cultures, may simply be thought of as a good sales pitch. Resist the urge to oversell an idea, product, or even yourself. Furthermore, when people gather to listen, don't be surprised if they start filling up the seats from the back of the auditorium and leave the front rows empty. Reluctance to occupy a prominent place is typically Finnish, and no reflection on you.

TEAMWORK

A Finn is naturally a loner. The pattern of early settlements in Finland was such that you would build your house on a hill near a waterway and your land would surround the house. Your neighbor would do

the same, so the distance from one house to another could be great. It is said that early settlers would be outraged if they saw wood shavings floating down the river past their house; this would inevitably mean that somebody had broken the rules and had settled too close to you. This may be a myth, but it certainly has more than a grain of truth.

The Finnish education system has sought to change this cultural resistance to teamwork, and it is now a staple of Finnish school and working life. Meetings in which people break off into smaller groups to discuss something or to tackle a problem are commonplace, as are company-wide seminars and training. In fact, you may end up doing far more teamwork in Finland than you ever cared to!

LEADERSHIP AND DECISION-MAKING

Decision-making is usually a democratic process in a Finnish company. Quick decisions are followed by prompt action, based on the principle that, if you are going to do something, you might as well get on with it.

Human rights and ecological issues are major factors in decision-making. Doubts about any possible environmental impact must be allayed. Finns have learned this the hard way. The cellulose and paper industry, back in the 1950s and 1960s, were big polluters, but there has been a total turnaround in this respect. Nowadays, the forestry industry is a good model of sustainable development.

Women and men are equal. In the past, the leaders of Finnish business and industry were all men, and many boardroom matters were discussed during sauna evenings. Firms still have saunas for entertaining clients, but this happens less now that there are so many female executives. These days you are more likely to be entertained by a round of golf or an evening at the opera.

Giving Gifts

When giving business gifts, make sure that you don't appear to be bribing anyone—bribery is unacceptable. With that said, Finns will warmly accept a gift from your home culture.

TIMING AND PUNCTUALITY

The Finns are known for their punctuality and promptness. Eight o'clock means 8:00, not 8:05. If you have called in an electrician, and he says he will be at your house at 8:00 a.m., it would not be unusual for him to arrive at 7:30 a.m., and Finns would expect this. Deliveries are usually made as arranged, and payments are made promptly. Theatrical and musical performances start on time, and people do not keep you waiting. Of course, there are always exceptions.

The twenty-four-hour clock is used for all official appointments and timetables. Finns also use the international week numbers. You may hear people saying, "I will be busy in week 5, but I can meet you in week 6." If, like many of us, these week numbers are largely meaningless to you, check your calendar, google it, or simply ask your colleague to give you the precise dates in question.

MEETINGS AND NEGOTIATIONS

The format of a meeting will be settled beforehand, and a formal meeting will have a chairman and an agenda. Finns don't like surprises—and they won't pull any on you either.

Business negotiations are sometimes carried out at the company sauna or on the golf course. The sauna evenings can get very jolly, with lots of alcohol consumed. If you have been invited to lunch, the Finn will let you know if he wants it to be a working lunch. Alcohol is not usually consumed at business lunches these days—long, convivial lunches are a thing of the past. Finns don't usually drink during the working day, but they will make up for it at the bar afterward. You can, however, expect to be offered coffee several times a day.

CONTRACTS

Finns rely on written contracts to ensure that rights are guaranteed and that agreements remain in place. This does not detract from the sincerity of verbal agreements, however, nor from their expectation of honesty in kind. Whether a contract is spoken or written, Finns are rule- and law-abiding, honest people, and they will adhere to agreements.

However, from a legal perspective, you should make sure that your contracts are explicit; the interpretation of contracts is usually based on precisely what is written there, rather than on legislation.

HANDLING DISAGREEMENTS

Finns are very determined, and they hold strong opinions, but many do not like confrontation. Give a Finn time to think. If there is a justifiable cause for complaint, he will pursue his case. When there is a disagreement, make your case calmly and rationally. If emotions are high, some Finns may decide that they would simply prefer to avoid you, or not to do business with you at all. However, if you make your case respectfully and rationally, most Finns will be very willing to work with you to reach a consensus.

WOMEN IN BUSINESS

Women occupy a strong role within Finnish society, and that includes business. Things aren't perfect; there is still a large majority of male board members and CEOs. However, women make up about 33 percent of these positions, and that percentage has risen every year since 2003.

If you are a businesswoman, you can (usually) expect to be treated as an equal in Finland. There is one awkward fact of life in the Finnish business world, however: the sauna! Finnish business people like to go for saunas together, yet Finnish social norms dictate that men and women should go

separately. This can result in some situations in which businesswomen find themselves excluded. If you find yourself in such a situation, you can insist on being invited to such gatherings and being allowed your own sauna turn. Finnish men are used to assertive women and shouldn't be bothered by this.

CHAPTER NINE

COMMUNICATING

LANGUAGE

Finnish (*suomi*) is a Finno-Ugrian language. It is generally considered to be difficult, but in fact it is very logical, and almost mathematical in its rules of inflection and conjugation. English-speakers find the language quite hard to learn, but only because it has very little in common with English—though more and more English loan words are entering the language all the time. Finns appreciate any effort on the part of a foreigner to speak Finnish, as they take pride in their language. Communicating with Finnish people and experiencing the culture in Finnish is an enriching experience, though not necessarily a straightforward one.

Both Finnish and Swedish are official languages in Finland, with 93 percent of Finns speaking Finnish as their mother tongue, and 5.6 percent speaking Swedish as theirs. All official communications from the state administration and national institutions appear in both languages. Everybody in Finland learns the other domestic language at school. The south and southwest of Finland are the main Swedish-speaking areas together with the Åland Islands, which are 99 percent Swedish-speaking. Finnish is also spoken in northern Sweden along the river Tornio, and by about 300,000 Finns living in Sweden. There are over a million Finns, or their descendants, outside Finland, many of them in the USA, Canada, and Australia.

The Sami languages *(saami)* are spoken by about 1,700 people in Lapland. When traveling around Finland it is worth noting that the road signs are usually in both Finnish and Swedish, particularly in the south and the west of the country. The Finnish name is written first where the majority language locally is Finnish, and Swedish where it is Swedish. In the Sami-speaking areas in the north, signs also appear in the local Sami dialect. Unfortunately, all of the Sami languages spoken in Finland are under threat of extinction. This is mostly due to the prevalence of Finnish and the increased use of English.

Many dialects of Finnish are spoken around the country, but they are all mutually intelligible, for the most part. The most obvious difference that exists between these dialects can be found in personal pronouns, which can differ a lot from area to area. If you want to sound native, one step in that direction is to start using the local pronouns!

There is also a distinct difference between the standard written language and the spoken language. Much like with dialects, the most obvious difference between spoken and written Finnish can be found in personal pronoun usage. Written pronouns include *minä* (I) and *sinä* (you), neither of which are used in spoken language, except in very official contexts. Other noticeable differences can be found in verb conjugation as well as in pronunciation.

Speaking English

Finns speak English very well, and Finland is among the countries in Europe with the highest general proficiency in the language. The Finnish education system has placed a lot of emphasis on teaching English to its citizens in an effort to prepare them for a globalized world. As such, surviving with only English is fairly easy, especially if you stick to areas with higher populations. Furthermore, if you find yourself in a professional, academic, or business context, it is certain that the people around you will have a high level of English.

You may notice some peculiarities in the way Finns use English, though. For one thing, the

Finnish language has a very flat intonation, making it sound somewhat monotone. This can mean that when they speak English their lack of inflection sounds emotionless or cold, or perhaps even angry. Secondly, Finns tend to use the imperative and avoid the conditional. In plain language, this means that it can seem odd or overly formal in Finnish to ask, "Would you like some coffee?" Instead, Finns prefer to say, "Have some coffee!" or "Take a bun!" This is also evident in e-mails, where an English speaker would probably use a bit more finesse in making requests by using the conditional "Would you?" and the word "please." Finns don't really have an exact equivalent for the word "please" and instead prefer to ask questions and make requests more directly. Keep these things in mind during any interactions you may have with Finns, and it will surely help to avoid misunderstandings.

When using a directory or a dictionary you need to remember that Finnish has three letters that do not appear in English: the Swedish *å* (pronounced as the "o" in "hot"), the letter *ä* (pronounced as the "a" in "hat"), and the letter *ö* (pronounced as the "er" in "herd"). They appear at the end of the alphabet. The letters *v* and *w* are interchangeable in Finnish.

If you plan to spend any length of time in Finland, though, learning some Finnish will help you understand the Finns and their culture in far more depth. If you have the time, learn some vocabulary, familiarize yourself with some basic grammar rules, or perhaps even take a class. Even if you never return to Finland, it won't be a waste of your time.

SILENCE

The Finns respect silence and are comfortable with it. Folk wisdom praises the virtue of silence as a sign of wisdom, and talkativeness as the sign of foolishness. In conversation there are moments of silence, when the Finn weighs up what has been said, before making his or her own contribution. In fact, to answer immediately would signify lack of respect for the views of the previous speaker. Silence at the dinner table does not bother the Finns, but it can feel very awkward to someone from the English-speaking world, who is accustomed to keeping the conversation flowing.

That said, however, there are those who would suggest that the notion of "the silent Finn" is exaggerated, even mythologized. Your personal experience will allow you to decide for yourself about Finnish silence and just how common it really is.

Silence is a Precious Commodity

A British travel writer, trekking in Lapland
with a Finnish guide, tells a story:
"We had walked for two days without seeing
anybody. Then I saw someone in the distance,
coming toward us, and really looked forward
to exchanging views about the beauty of
Lapland in the full glow of autumn colors.
The man came closer and closer, passed us
with barely a nod, and continued on his way. I
turned to my guide to ask why we didn't stop
to talk. The guide explained that this man
would have come to the wilderness to enjoy
the silence and to be alone, and that we had no
right to disturb him."

BODY LANGUAGE

Finns are very serious and attentive when they
are listening to you. They do not always smile
a great deal, and there is very little overt body
language, maybe a little nodding in agreement or
interjections like "*hmm,*" "*jaa-a,*" "*juu,*" "*oho,*" "*voi
voi,*" and "*aij jai.*" Some avoid eye contact because
they are shy, but Finns are taught to look people
in the eye, and it is considered good manners to
do so.

The Finns are fond of making speeches. It is customary to make a speech at a birthday party, wedding, or other special occasion, or sometimes just to make an occasion special. There is a very marked difference after a few drinks, when Finns definitely liven up and come out of their shells!

Handshakes are always expected when you greet someone for the first time, and also on departure. Young people do not usually shake hands among themselves, and when they are introduced they often just nod and exchange greetings. It is customary to hug close friends and family when you meet them after a long separation.

CONVERSATION

Finns enjoy exchanging views with others. Small talk doesn't come easily to them, but this doesn't mean that they don't like talking. The pace can be slow, and pauses are natural. Some Finns speak particularly slowly when they speak English. Silence, when considering what has been said, is expected and accepted. Responses can take a long time to come.

A common topic of conversation is the weather. The Finnish climate provides plenty to talk about. A few remarks about the weather are exchanged at the start of many conversations, such as, "Have you seen the weather forecast?" Finns like to gossip like everybody else. Sports and TV programs are typical topics of conversation, as are politics and people in the public eye.

Finns are taught not to interrupt someone who is speaking. Sometimes the slow pace of speech leads a foreign listener to think that the Finn has stopped, and he or she starts to speak, to the annoyance of the Finn who was only pausing to think.

Finns also talk about money—at least other people's money—along with prices and wages; even illnesses and medication are common topics at the coffee table.

Forms of Address

The Finnish language has the formal and informal address, like French and German. *Sinä* is the informal "you," and *Te* is the formal. There used to be strict social rules about who could use the informal address to whom, and who was allowed to suggest being on first-name terms. Nowadays people are very informal. After being introduced you are usually invited to use first names, and it is perfectly acceptable to do so. If you do speak some Finnish, you should feel comfortable using the informal, except with the very elderly and in extremely formal situations.

When you introduce yourself, it is common to say your first name first and then your surname, but on a list of participants or guests it is common to have the surname first followed by the first name.

People are not as concerned with titles as they used to be. but if you want be deferential you can use titles like *tohtori*, doctor, or *professori*, professor. If you are doing business with Finns, you can always check the protocol with them—it is better to ask than to cause offense. The words for Mr. (*herra*), Mrs. (*rouva*), and Miss (*neiti*) are used only in very formal contexts, and other than that, almost never. The press commonly refers to public figures just by their surnames or title and surname, such as Niinistö or Presidentti Niinistö when talking about the current president.

Most Finnish companies have a policy of using first names with all colleagues. Schoolchildren address their teachers by their first names. Generally, the style of Finnish address is informal and not hierarchical, mirroring some aspects of their society and values.

Greetings

When you see someone first thing in the morning you say "*Hyvää huomenta*" ("Good morning"). Later on and through the day you can say "*Hyvää päivää*" ("Good day!"). In the evening you can say "*Hyvää iltaa*" ("Good evening"), although this is rarely used outside formal contexts. All of these are answered by repeating the greeting back. When you leave you can say "*hei hei*" ("Good-bye").

The greetings "*Hei!*" and "*Moi!*" both mean "Hello!" and can be used at any time of the day.

"*Kiitos*" means "thank you"; "*Ole hyvä*" means "you're welcome."

When you go into a shop or bar, you may be asked "*Mitä sinä otat?*" ("What can I get you?") You can say "*Haluaisin . . .*," or "*Otan . . .*," which means "I would like. . ." You can say your order in English and hope that you have a sales assistant who understands, or you can start by asking "*Puhutko englantia?*" ("Do you speak English?"). If someone has gone out of their way to help you, you can say "*Kiitos avusta!*" ("Thank you for your help.") Another useful phrase is "*Voisitko sanoa . . .?*" ("Could you tell me . . .?")

HUMOR

Most Finns have a good sense of humor. Finnish is very rich and expressive and there are many words for different kinds of laughter. Much of the humor is based on puns and playing with words. Finns like both crazy humor and subtle, dry humor, and are very good at cryptic self-irony. When life is tough, you need to laugh to get through it. Finns laugh at themselves but they are not pleased if you laugh at them. They love telling jokes and funny stories. Sex is often a source of humor, because it is still slightly taboo, and it is easier to deal with this by joking about it. Politics, politicians, and current affairs are all fair game for satire.

So what makes the Finns laugh? Popular TV programs include classic American sitcoms, such as *Frasier*, *Friends*, *Sex and the City*, and *How I Met Your Mother*, and many British comedy programs, such as *Mr. Bean* and *Yes, Prime Minister*. Risqué stories and jokes—particularly about the Swedes and the Russians—are relished, but their translation into English doesn't usually work.

Well known Finnish comedian, Ismo Leikola, was given the distinction of being named "Funniest Man in The World" in 2014. His humor is a good example of the effective intersection between what appeals to Finns and what appeals to Anglophones. Whether in Finnish or English, Leikola jokes a lot about language and the oddities found therein.

> ### Can I Help You?
> Another joke from Ismo Leikola: about his time in America, he said that it took him a very long time to learn "that 'Can I help you?' actually means 'Go away!'"

WRITTEN COMMUNICATIONS

The Finns are not great letter writers, and written confirmation is not always sent: a verbal communication is often enough. Finns don't go back on their word.

Be aware that the language used in written communications may be very short and abrupt. Only the essence of the message is written, and there are no flourishes. In fact, the short-and-to-the-point style of e-mail suits the Finns perfectly.

SERVICES

The Internet and Media
Nearly all of Finland is well connected to the Internet, both via Wi-Fi and speedy cellular data connections. As in many cultures these days, Finns consume much of their media through their smartphones and other mobile devices.

Watching conventional broadcast television and cable is a common pastime, but so are subscriptions to streaming services. Regardless of how and what you're watching, all foreign-language content is subtitled rather than dubbed. The public television channels are run by the Finnish Broadcasting Company, which also publishes a lot of news articles and other online content. In fact, you can access nearly all of what these channels air on TV through an app called Yle Areena. If you're interested in learning Finnish, you ought to take a look.

Cell Phones

Finland is the promised land of cell phones. In fact, landlines are no longer used at all, except in some businesses or telemarketing firms. "*Matkapuhelin*" is the official Finnish word for a cell phone, but the common word in everyday language is "*kännykkä*," literally, "something that fits the palm of your hand."

If you're in the market for a prepaid SIM card, they are quite easy to obtain from network shops such as DNA, Elisa, and Telia.

Mail

The Finnish postal service is called Posti, and, like most Finnish services, they are reliable. Their logo reads "Posti" in bright orange, so if you're looking to send a postcard or a package, you can't miss it.

Posti is generally open from 8:00 a.m. to 8.00 p.m., Monday through Friday, from 10:00 a.m. to 3:00 p.m.

on Saturdays, and closed on Sundays. In addition to Posti, you can purchase stamps at grocery stores and small shops.

CONCLUSION

The Finns are a resilient and independent people. The enduring communal spirit and indomitable *sisu* that saw them through centuries of foreign rule continue to shape their society today. The progress of the past hundred years or so means they are very much at home in the global village, yet their roots are firmly planted in Finnish soil.

Most Finns today live in cities; however their connection to the countryside and to nature remains strong. The landscape is beautiful, often breathtakingly so, and the people appreciate its beauty throughout the seasons.

Indeed, there is much to be enjoyed in Finland. Business is thriving. The music scene is excellent. Arts and design permeate the whole society. The architecture varies from medieval stone churches to modern icons of cutting-edge design. Then there is the great outdoors—whatever time of year you decide to visit, you'll have numerous opportunities to enjoy the natural beauty, whether on foot, in canoe, or in skis. You will never want for modern conveniences, but going off the grid for a while is easy, too.

Don't let the notion of "Finnish silence" scare you. The Finns might be a little more hesitant to speak up or to demand attention than others, but they are kind and are generally interested in people from other places. And should you happen to run into an especially "silent Finn," why not enjoy the silence?

This Nordic gem is very much a part of Europe, but is one of the most remote, spacious, and beautiful corners of the continent. Its remarkable land is a joy to explore, and its creative, fair-minded, and resilient people are well worth getting to know.

FURTHER READING

Boyle, Max. *The Honest Tribe: Travels in Finland*. Leicester: Troubador Publishing Ltd, 2018.

Korhonen, Karoliina. *Finnish Nightmares: An Irreverent Guide to Life's Awkward Moments*. Berkeley: Ten Speed Press, 2019.

Nenye, Vesa, Peter Munter, et al. *Finland at War: The Winter War 1939–40*. Oxford: Osprey Publishing, 2018.

Nylund, Joanna. *Sisu: The Finnish Art of Courage*. Pennsylvania: Running Press, 2018.

Pantzar, Katja. T*he Finnish Way: Finding Courage, Wellness, and Happiness Through the Power of Sisu*. New York: TarcherPerigee, 2018

Partanen, Anu. *The Nordic Theory of Everything: In Search of a Better Life*. New York: Harper Paperbacks, 2017.

Rantanen, Miska. *Pantsdrunk: Kalsarikanni: The Finnish Path to Relaxation*. New York: Harper Design, 2018.

Tuomainen, Antti, David Hackston. *Palm Beach, Finland*. London: Orenda Books, 2019.

Vaananen-Jensen, Inkeri, Deb Schense, et al. *Finnish Proverbs*. Iowa: Penfield Books, 2012.

Walker, Timothy. T*each Like Finland: 33 Strategies for a Joyful Classroom*. New York: W. W. Norton & Company, 2017.

PICTURE CREDITS